the knot
book of
wedding
lists

Copyright © 2007
The Knot, Inc.

All rights reserved.
Published in the United States
by CLARKSON POTTER/PUBLISHERS,
an imprint of the
CROWN PUBLISHING GROUP,
a division of RANDOM HOUSE, Inc., New York.
www.crownpublishing.com
www.clarksonpotter.com

CLARKSON N. POTTER is a trademark and POTTER
and colophon are registered trademarks of
Random House, Inc.

Library of Congress Cataloging-in-Publication Data
Roney, Carley.
The Knot book of wedding lists / by Carley Roney and
the editors of The Knot. — 1st ed.
1. Weddings—Planning.   I. Knot (Firm)   II. Title.
HQ745.R647   2007
395.2'2—dc22   2007027756
ISBN 978-0-307-34193-8
Printed in the U.S.A.

DESIGN BY JENNIFER K. BEAL
ILLUSTRATIONS BY JASON O'MALLEY

26   28   30   29   27   25

First Edition

the knot
book of
wedding
lists
**The Ultimate Guide
to the Perfect Day, Down
to the Smallest Detail**

CARLEY RONEY
and the editors of TheKnot.com

Clarkson/Potter Publishers
New York

contents

a note from
the knot

at the knot, we love lists!

Everything seems more doable when broken down into bullets. And the sense of accomplishment, as you check the little boxes, can't be beat. Chapter by chapter, this book transforms the perplexing process of planning a wedding into a series of simple task lists. We make it easy for you to pick your color scheme, decide on a menu, and even choose your gown. So grab a pen, start at the beginning, and get checking. But first, here are the five things you need to know about this book:

- **You don't need all the answers now.**
  Each section starts with questions and fresh ideas to help you conceptualize your wedding look.

- **You'll learn to talk like a pro.**
  With smart questions to ask and contract points to push, we help you hire the right professionals to help you pull it off.

- **We won't leave you hanging.**
  The last chapter outlines the decisions and final to-dos to keep you on track right down to your wedding day.

- **Don't be intimidated.**
  There are many to-dos—more than 500, to be exact—but we promise we'll make you feel like a seasoned veteran, in control and unintimidated.

- **You can fast-track it.**
  Do Chapter 2 (The Reception) and Chapter 3 (The Ceremony) right away—these are the most important.

month-by-month timeline

12+ months

- ☐ Set a date.
- ☐ Determine your wedding day style and colors.
- ☐ Hire a wedding planner. (FIND OUT WHAT TO LOOK FOR IN CHAPTER 1: THE WEDDING PLAN.)
- ☐ Set up a budget.
- ☐ Compile your final guest list.
- ☐ Create a web page to announce your wedding.
- ☐ Choose your wedding party. (GET THE DOS AND DON'TS IN CHAPTER 7: THE WEDDING PARTY.)
- ☐ Have an engagement party.
- ☐ Book your ceremony and reception locations.
- ☐ Book your officiant.

9–11 months

- ☐ Send out save-the-date cards. (FIND OUT WHAT ELSE TO ORDER IN CHAPTER 8: THE INVITATIONS AND STATIONERY.)
- ☐ Book your caterer.
- ☐ Book your entertainment. (GET TIPS ON FINDING THE BEST DJ OR BAND IN CHAPTER 13: THE ENTERTAINMENT.)
- ☐ Book your florist. (SEE THE BEST FLOWERS FOR YOUR WEDDING DATE IN CHAPTER 9: THE FLOWERS AND DÉCOR.)
- ☐ Book your photographer and videographer. (LEARN WHAT TO ASK IN CHAPTER 11: THE PHOTOGRAPHY AND VIDEOGRAPHY.)

6–8 months

- ☐ Buy your gown. (GET GOWN KNOW-HOW IN CHAPTER 12: THE GOWN.)
- ☐ Determine your menu. (LEARN YOUR OPTIONS IN CHAPTER 4: THE MENU.)
- ☐ Book your cake baker. (FIND THE CAKE LINGO IN CHAPTER 10: THE WEDDING CAKE.)
- ☐ Book your transportation. (GET EVERYONE ROLLING IN CHAPTER 14: THE TRANSPORTATION.)
- ☐ Book your ceremony musicians. (FIGURE OUT WHAT THEY'LL PLAY IN CHAPTER 3: THE CEREMONY.)
- ☐ Buy bridesmaid dresses.
- ☐ Register for gifts. (DECIDE WHAT TO REGISTER FOR IN CHAPTER 15: THE GIFT REGISTRY.)

4–5 months

- ☐ Make honeymoon arrangements. (SEE WHERE TO GO IN CHAPTER 16: THE HONEYMOON.)
- ☐ Rent or buy formalwear.
- ☐ Order your invitations. (LEARN WHAT ELSE GOES INTO THE ENVELOPE IN CHAPTER 8: THE INVITATIONS AND STATIONERY.)
- ☐ Order your wedding bands.
- ☐ Hire a calligrapher, if using.
- ☐ Reserve tables, chairs, and/or other rental equipment you'll need.

month-by-month timeline

3 months

- ☐ Finalize the guest list.
- ☐ Appoint ushers and other ceremony helpers.
- ☐ Mail out invitations.
- ☐ Book your hairstylist and makeup artist. (GET BEAUTY KNOW-HOW IN CHAPTER 12: THE GOWN.)
- ☐ Decide on and buy accessories for wedding party.
- ☐ Finalize postwedding brunch details, if having one.
- ☐ Finalize rehearsal dinner details. (SEE ALL THE DETAILS IN CHAPTER 7: THE WEDDING PARTY.)

1–2 months

- ☐ Discuss your vows—will you write your own or recite traditional ones?
- ☐ Purchase gifts for parents, attendants, and other special guests.
- ☐ Have your final gown fitting.
- ☐ Order welcome baskets. (DECIDE WHAT WILL GO IN THEM IN CHAPTER 5: THE GUESTS)
- ☐ Have your wedding shower and/or bachelor/bachelorette party.
- ☐ Order favors. (GET IDEAS ON WHAT TO GIVE IN CHAPTER 2: THE RECEPTION.)
- ☐ Have your bridal shower. (GET A CHECKLIST IN CHAPTER 6: THE WEDDING PARTY.)
- ☐ Finalize your floral proposal. (GET PROPOSAL TIPS IN CHAPTER 8: THE FLOWERS AND DÉCOR.)

1-2 weeks

- [ ] Apply for a marriage license.
- [ ] Call guests who haven't RSVP'd.
- [ ] Assemble day-of emergency kit (MAID OF HONOR COULD DO THIS).
- [ ] Determine day-of assignments for the wedding party.
- [ ] Call location manager and make sure your vendors have access to the site when they need it.
- [ ] Finalize seating chart and get it to reception site manager. (GET SEATING HELP IN CHAPTER 2: THE RECEPTION.)
- [ ] Check in with all vendors and confirm all details.
- [ ] Assemble or package favors. (GET IDEAS IN CHAPTER 2: THE RECEPTION.)

3-7 days

- [ ] Rent your formalwear.
- [ ] Have your rehearsal dinner.
- [ ] Finalize all transportation details.
- [ ] Pack for your honeymoon.
- [ ] Set aside tips for your vendors.

the
wedding
plan

chapter 1

Once the excitement of your engagement settles, you realize that it's time to plan the wedding (that's why you're using this book, right?). Don't get overwhelmed. The trick to pulling it all together is getting organized, staying grounded, and maintaining your overall vision.

creating your wedding plan

The secret to a gorgeous wedding is a definitive style and color scheme. And though carrying it through all the wedding day details may at first seem overwhelming, just take it one element at a time. To begin envisioning your perfect wedding day, you need to make some big-picture decisions. Decide the date (springtime, fall, winter?); the location (at home, in a ballroom, at a restaurant?); how formal it will be (sit-down dinner, laid-back brunch?); and the colors you'll use. Once you've done this, all other style details will fall into place. So let's get started.

→ when do we want our wedding to take place?

Whether fall is your favorite because of the foliage or you love spring because of the gardens, decide the season of your wedding and then settle on a month.

→ where do we want to have our wedding/reception?

You may have decided long ago that your reception would take place at your favorite museum, or that you want all your family to gather for a reception at the country club. If you're set on a particular location, use it to inspire the rest of your wedding day details. Some locations to consider:

- Ballroom/hotel
- Country club
- Your home
- Restaurant
- Garden
- Beach
- Mountaintop
- Loft
- Yacht club
- Art gallery
- Flower shop

Shortcut: TheKnot.com/wedding style

→ how formal will our wedding be?

Decide whether you're after a formal affair or a casual wedding, or something in between. And consider dress code here: Will your guests wear tuxes and floor-length dresses? Or will it be more laid-back?

- Formal/black-tie (an evening wedding—tuxes or jackets for the guys and floor-length dresses for the ladies)
- Semiformal (a late-afternoon or evening wedding—ties but no jackets for the guys; cocktail attire for the ladies)
- Casual/laid-back (an anytime affair—ties-optional for the guys, and sandals and laid-back dresses and skirts for the ladies)

→ what colors do we want to use?

If you have a favorite color, by all means use it on your wedding day to reflect your personalities. Carry your colors through from the invitations to the flowers, bridesmaid dresses, and reception décor for a unified look. If you're in need of a little color direction, choose one main color and an accent color, or two equally prominent complementary colors. Some hot color combos:

- Orange and pink
- Green and blue
- Black and white
- Yellow and cream
- Purple and brown
- Turquoise and red

→ what's our style?

From a traditional country club wedding to a modern loft affair, there are many ways to define your wedding day. Your reception site, colors, and the time of day will reflect your style. Some ideas include:

- **Traditional** (at a country club, traditional gown and colors)
- **Modern** (in a loft, sleek centerpieces, and a tall modern cake)

- **Intimate** (at home, at a winery, or a restaurant)
- **Glamorous** (totally over-the-top, from the centerpieces to a five-course menu)
- **Theme** (use a favorite city or hobby to inspire all the wedding day details)
- **Cultural** (a black-and-red banquet-style affair for a Chinese wedding)
- **Beach** (a seaside affair with nautical elements and blues and greens)
- **Destination** (in Italy or the Bahamas; a vacation for guests)

→ what's our budget?

You need to ask all contributing parties (bride's parents, groom's parents, yourselves), how much they are willing to put into the wedding fund. Your budget will dictate many of your wedding decisions.

→ what are our priorities?

Together, decide the three most important elements of the wedding day for each of you. That's where you could give a little more money and attention. And, it will help make divvying up responsibilities easier. If he is all about the music, let him scope out possible bands and DJs. If you want a couture gown, you might have to opt for a less expensive invitation.

→ how involved will the groom be?

To avoid the I'm-doing-everything fight later, set expectations now for how the groom should be included.

→ who's got the final say?

It's tricky when multiple parties are helping to cover the wedding costs, but the ultimate decisions should be yours. Subtly make this known early on, again, to avoid hurt feelings later.

→ do we want a wedding planner/event coordinator?

Though this book will cover everything thoroughly, keep reading for all the information on the different roles a planner can assume and the best ways to work together. If you know you don't need or want the help, turn to Chapter 2 to get started on the reception.

finding a wedding planner

Planning, organizing, and carrying out a unique and gorgeous wedding takes exceptional skill—and you'll want to make sure you find the right person for the job. There are lots of things to consider when choosing a planning pro.

→ do we want to hire a professional planner?

Reasons you might want a planner:

- To save you time. A consultant can take on a large or small amount of responsibility and can also cut out some of the early research and legwork.
- To plan a destination wedding. It's highly recommended you hire a planner if your wedding is far away—there are tons of extra details to arrange.
- To get extras and possible discounts based on their knowledge of the industry and relationships with various vendors.
- To have a wedding expert on hand to answer all your planning questions.
- To have a referee for family disputes.
- To have someone there the day of the wedding to make sure the day goes off without a hitch.

{ your budget breakdown }

Before you sign on any dotted lines or pay any deposits, you'll need to create a budget. Consider this average percentage breakdown:

Reception and Rentals—48%

Reception site
Tent
Food
Wedding cake
Alcohol
Tables
Chairs
Tableware
Flatware
Glassware
Linens
Dance floor
Lighting
Other add-ins (Ice bar, photo booth, portable bathrooms)
Gratuity (for bartenders, waitstaff, and coat check)

Ceremony—3%

Ceremony site
Officiant fee/donation
Marriage license
Special décor (unity candle, chuppah)

Wedding Rings—3%

Stationery—3%

Save-the-date cards
Invitations
Calligrapher
Ceremony programs
Guest book

Escort cards

Place cards

Menu cards

Napkins

Boxes or tags for favors

Announcements

Thank-you cards

Stamps

Flowers—8%

Bridal bouquet

Bridesmaid bouquets

Boutonnieres

Parent/grandparent corsages

Flowers for flower girl

Corsages for readers, candle lighter, and ushers

Ceremony flowers

Centerpieces

Cake flowers

Delivery and gratuity

Photography and Videography—12%

Engagement photos

Photographer for ceremony/reception

Prints

Album

Videographer for ceremony/reception

DVDs

continued...

Wedding Attire—10%

Gown/groom's formalwear

Alterations

Veil/headpiece

Shoes

Lingerie

Purse

Accessories

Hair and makeup

Entertainment—8%

Ceremony musicians

Cocktail-hour musicians/DJ

Reception musicians/DJ/band

Other special music (drummers, dancers, pianist)

Transportation and Accommodations—2%

Transportation for the wedding party

Transportation for the guests

Parking

Hotel rooms

Gratuity (drivers and concierges)

Gifts—3%

Bride's attendants

Groom's attendants

Parents of bride

Parents of groom

Other wedding attendants (readers, ushers)

Favors

** Wedding Planner—10%

If you use an event consultant, add an extra 10 percent of your wedding budget to the total cost.

☐ determine what role your planner will play.

There are three basic levels of involvement.

- Plans and coordinates the entire event from start to finish (from overall vision to weekend activities). This type of planner typically charges a flat fee.
- Helps you shape the event by giving you décor suggestions, vendor recommendations, or assistance with specific projects—you contact the planner when you need help. Charges either an hourly rate or a flat fee.
- Acts as a day-of coordinator to make sure the wedding day runs smoothly. Also organizes final details like the ceremony rehearsal and wedding day deliveries. Charges a flat fee.

☐ gather names of local planners.

- Use local magazines and city guides at TheKnot.com/local, to find the names of planners in your area. Vendors who advertise to brides take their businesses very seriously.
- If you have a reception site, ask your reception site manager for wedding planner suggestions.
- Ask friends who have recently married—and were pleased with their weddings—for the names of their planners.

☐ check out prospective planners' websites.

Look for photos of recent weddings. Notice whether the elements seem to have a cohesive look and if there's an overarching style that the weddings share—this is probably what the planner is most experienced with, so decide if it is one you like. Additional information you should look for:

- Types of planning services offered
- Names of sites they've worked with
- Awards
- Membership in professional associations (such as the Association of Bridal Consultants)
- Testimonials from recent clients

☐ call your favorite two or three to make an appointment. but first confirm the following:

- Wedding date availability.
- Appropriateness, pricewise. Ask their typical price range and/or the cost of the average wedding they plan.
- Services offered (day of, event planning, partial planning).

☐ prepare for your meeting.

Bring the following with you to the interview:

- Planner's address and phone number (just in case)
- Your budget (at least some general guidelines)
- Photos of décor, colors, gowns (anything to express your style and ideas)
- List of questions and a notepad for taking notes

☐ meet with planners.

At your meeting, you obviously want to get a sense of the quality of his or her weddings, but you are also looking for his or her personal qualities: Is this someone you can work with intimately for months at a time? To break the ice, ask:

- How long have you been a wedding planner?
- How many weddings do you plan a year?
- What was the most unique wedding you ever planned?

☐ check out his or her portfolio.

Again, make sure his style suits your taste. If all the weddings that he has planned look over-the-top and glamorous and you're looking for a small intimate gathering, he may not be the right person for you. That said, a planner's job is to make a couple's vision a reality, so you'll want to make sure that you communicate well together.

☐ express your ideas.

Voice your ideas about your style and colors and see how the planner responds—your ideas should be met with enthusiasm. And a planner should be able to listen to your ideas and hone them, making your wedding something truly unique and memorable. Ask:

- Are there specific vendors you like to use?
- Do you create the overall vision, or are you more a producer who brings in an event designer?
- What of the following do you handle?

    ☐ Event styling
    ☐ Vendor services
    ☐ Vendor contracts
    ☐ Guest list coordination
    ☐ RSVPs
    ☐ Payment processing
    ☐ Destination weddings
    ☐ Day-of coordination
    ☐ Rentals

- What is really your specialty, styling or coordinating? (Event designers focus on pulling together the overall look of the day rather than organizing all the myriad details.)

☐ ask about pricing and how the relationship will work.

There are so many ways you can work with a planner. Each one will have her own payment structure and preferred type of communication (e-mail, weekly phone calls, in-person reviews). If necessary, ask:

- How do payments work? (A percentage of our budget? A flat fee?)
- How many meetings will we have?
- What are the steps we'll go through?
- Do you come with us to all relevant meetings?
- How many options will you present for our vendors (florists, photographers)?
- Have you planned any other weddings at our site?
- Are you offered client discounts from any vendors that you work with?
- What is the process for selecting and hiring vendors?

- Will there be additional expenses on top of your base fee? (Travel, parking, food?)
- What's the best way to get in contact with you?
- How many people on your staff will be at the wedding?
- What happens if you are ill on our wedding day?
- Do you have references? (You may want to ask for both professional—like reception sites—and recent brides.)

booking your wedding planner

Don't feel pressured to hire your planner on the spot. Give yourself time to compare and contrast prices, impressions, notes, and if provided, a formal proposal. (Some planners may draft their overall vision for your wedding and their intended services in the form of a proposal, which would then work as the basis for your contract.)

☐ call references and be sure to get a sense of the overall working relationship. you could ask:

- What was your wedding budget? How closely did the planner stay on budget?
- Can you e-mail me photos of your wedding? (This is a good way to confirm the overall consistency and professionalism of the wedding.)
- How well did the planner interpret your ideas?
- Was the style and wedding day exactly what you wanted?
- What did the planner take care of for you (guest list, vendor meetings, setup)?
- How many meetings did you have?
- Did she coordinate with other vendors and have good recommendations?
- Did the planner respond quickly to your calls or e-mails? Was he nice to work with?
- How was the staff on the wedding day?
- Did anything go wrong? How did your planner take care of the situation?
- Did the event go smoothly according to your guests?

☐ choose a planner and call immediately to express your desire to move forward.

☐ have your planner prepare a contract. be sure it includes:

- Your names and contact information (address, phone, and e-mail)
- Your event date
- Planner's company name and contact information (address, phone, and e-mail)
- Type of services you are engaging them for
- Total cost of services
- Expenses to be covered
- Deposit amount
- Payments to be made, in what form, and dates due
- To whom checks should be made out
- Cancellation and refund policy
- Planner's signature
- Your signatures

☐ send in your contract and put down your deposit at this time.

☐ pay the amount in full by the date agreed upon in the contract.

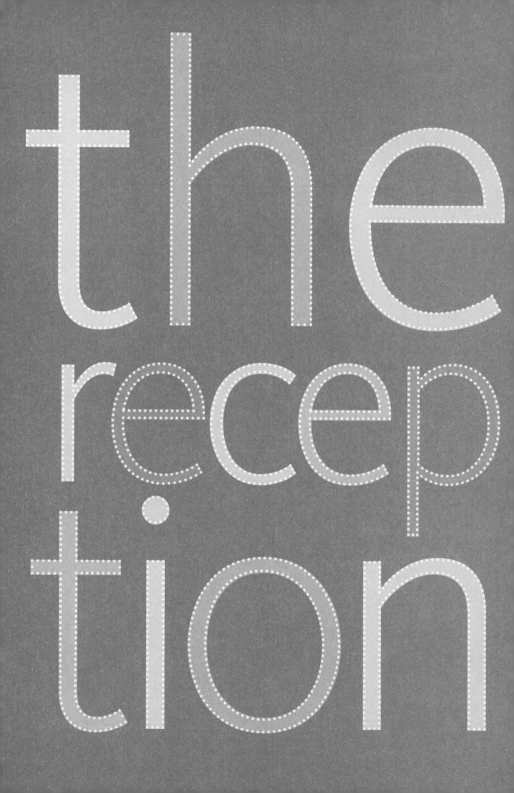

{ chapter 2 }

Want to know a little secret? Weddings aren't
just about getting married—they're about
showing off your style. That's why choosing
your reception site is one of the most important
and exciting wedding decisions you'll make. So
what should you look for, aside from that sense
of rightness you know you'll have the moment
you see the perfect spot? Charm, personality,
depth, and more than just a pretty face
(although looks do count!).

researching reception sites

- Know your wedding day style
- Know your approximate guest count
- Know your wedding date

Before you start scoping out possible sites, think about what you want in your ultimate location: Blank walls (a loft) or ready-made design (hotel ballroom)? Indoors or out? For inspiration, browse photos at TheKnot.com/realweddings, where you can search real weddings by style, area, and season. Then, consider the following questions:

→ **how many people do we need our space to accommodate?**

If you have close to three hundred guests coming, a cozy restaurant is out of the question, while a large ballroom will swallow up a close-knit group of friends and family.

→ **what's most important to us about the location?**

- Walking distance from the ceremony
- Within minutes of the ceremony site
- Indoors/outdoors
- By the water
- Surrounded by nature
- Best in the evening or in the daylight
- Gorgeous interiors/exteriors

→ **how much space does the site need to provide?**

- Dressing room for changing and getting hair and makeup done
- Ceremony space
- Cocktail hour space
- Outdoor tent
- After-party space
- Photo-taking locations (indoors and out)

→ **what other reception essentials will be provided?**

- Everything: chairs, china, tableware, catering, waitstaff, flowers, music
- Rentals (e.g., china and chairs), waitstaff, and catering
- Rentals only
- Nothing—we want to work with a raw space

→ do we want an exclusively outdoor space?

- What will our backup plan be in case of inclement weather? (Tent? Move everyone indoors?)
- What will the foliage look like on the wedding day?
- Will an outdoor site potentially affect allergies?
- How will we combat insects?
- Will the ground be level for tables and a dance floor?

→ do we want to host the wedding at home?

- Is there enough space to accommodate our guest list?
- Will we need to make any large home improvements or do any landscaping?
- What items will we need to rent, and how much of an expense will this add?
- How will we organize parking?
- Do we have enough bathrooms, or will we have to rent portable toilets?
- Will we need a generator for the band? Will the caterer need to bring in a kitchen?

→ do we want a tent? (if not, skip to page 19)

→ is there enough outdoor space for a tent?

To calculate the space needed, multiply the number of people coming to the wedding by 13 for the minimum size in square feet, or by 15 for the optimum. For example: 50 guests x 13 = 650 square feet; 50 guests x 15 = 750 square feet. So a comfortable range for 50 guests would be 650–750 square feet. Here's a cheat sheet:

NUMBER OF GUESTS	SIZE OF TENT (IN SQUARE FEET)
50	650–750
100	1,300–1,500
150	1,950–2,250
200	2,600–3,000
250	3,250–3,750
300	3,900–4,500

→ what type of tent do we want?

- Century (has sides with windows and one or several peaks—it can be a pole or a frame tent)
- Pole (has poles that line the perimeter as well as down the center; has to be staked into the ground)
- Frame (has poles along the perimeter; supported by the frame, not the poles)

→ what type of floor do we want?

Flooring is important—if you don't have one put in, you'll end up with wobbly tables and chairs. On top of that, if it rains, your guests will have to deal with the possibility of mud. Your options:

- Wood floors
- Vinyl floors
- Checkerboard floors

→ do we need air-conditioning or heat lamps?

Is your locale notorious for being a little chilly or too hot during the month you'll marry?

→ what kind of lighting do we want?

This is key to setting the ambiance of the tent.

- Paper lanterns
- Chandeliers

WAYS TO SAVE

The reception is your biggest wedding expense: Figure about 48–50 percent of your total budget since this often includes the food, alcohol, waitstaff, and site fee (the core elements of a wedding). Here's how to save:

- Trim the guest list. The only way to save significant wedding dollars is to cut the guest list. If you're spending $100 per person, cutting the guest list by fifty will save you $5,000.

- Marry on an off night. Friday and Sunday night weddings will cost you slightly less than the ever-popular Saturday night.

- Ask about discounts. Does your site have a slow season? If so, you might be able to get a deal.

- Find a site that's decorated. Love the look of poinsettias and tiny white lights? Find a hotel that's dressed up for the holidays to avoid bringing in extra floral arrangements.

{ the knot book of wedding lists

- Twinkle lights (strings of tiny lights)
- Gobo lighting (projected patterns on the walls or dance floor)
- Pin-spot lighting (a spotlight on one element)
- Wash lighting (colored lighting on a large area)

finding reception sites

Once you've nailed down your reception criteria, start seeking out sites. Since so many of the other decisions depend on the reception site, you'll want to begin the process early to guarantee your favorite spot. Here's a run-down of the steps to take:

☐ gather names of local reception sites.

- Use local magazines and city guides at TheKnot.com/local to browse for stylish sites.
- If you've chosen a ceremony space, ask them for ideas.
- Ask your planner (or other pros) for suggestions.
- If they were happy with their selection, ask recently married friends for the names of their reception sites.
- Ask friends and family members about great weddings they've attended, and where they were.

☐ check out prospective reception sites online.

Look for photos of recent weddings. Notice what type of décor is most often used—this is probably what the reception site is best at preparing, so make sure you like the look. Additional information to note:

- A list of provided services
- Names of vendors they work with
- Awards
- Testimonials from recent clients
- Any standout policies (no loud music, no outside vendors, curfews)

☐ narrow down your choices to three.

Look online for reviews of the sites you are leaning toward. And ask your planner (if you have one) whether they have strong feelings about a particular venue on your list.

☐ call sites to make an appointment. but first confirm the following:

- Wedding date availability. Many reception sites have a limit on the number of weddings they can host in a weekend.
- Appropriateness, pricewise. Ask their typical price range and/or cost of the average wedding they host.
- Customization capabilities. If you want to bring in décor, food, or alcohol, confirm that the site will allow it.

interviewing the site managers

Think of the site manager as the gatekeeper of your reception site. Unless you have a wedding planner, he or she will be responsible for helping you secure all the details of the day—or at least the delivery of those details. At your meeting, you'll want to check out the site itself, and also assess the professionalism of the reception manager and staff. Communication and comfort should be deciding factors as well.

☐ bring the following with you to the interview:

- Reception site address, phone number, contact name
- Your budget (at least a general guideline)
- The list of questions below and a notepad so you can refer back to their answers to make your final decision.

☐ look over the reception space.

Check out the space itself, and a portfolio of events in the space to get a feel for the range of ways it can look. Overall, you are looking to make sure the style suits your taste. (If you are looking for modern and the walls are clad with ornate décor, it's not a good fit.) And do the following:

- Picture yourself and all your guests in the space.
- Decide whether it makes your feel comfortable.
- Note whether the space seems to come alive at night and how it looks with décor and flowers.

☐ get a sense of the overall style. are they open to change? ask:

- Do you have styles to choose from? Can we alter them?
- Can we completely customize our service options?
- What do you think would be appropriate for our [insert style keywords] wedding?
- Are there any restrictions or rules about entertainment, decorations, or a dress code?

☐ find out some key space logistics. ask yourself (or the manager!):

- Does the style of the space match the look we're going for?
- Does the décor coordinate with our color scheme?
- Is there an echo in the room? This will affect how the band/DJ will sound.
- Do we like the view and the surrounding area?
- Where does the band/entertainment set up?
- Where do the buffet tables go? The cake table?
- Can we see sample floor plans and/or visit when the room is set up for a wedding, so we can see what everything looks like when it's set up?

☐ ask the nitty-gritty business questions. you know, the ones that will impact the price.

- How does the place charge—per person, by the hour, or flat fee? What is the payment plan?
- Does the location provide everything we'll need (tables, chairs, dinnerware, linens, stage for DJ or band, dance floor, tent, additional lighting, etc.)?

RENTAL CHECKLIST

Ask your reception site what will be included, and if these things aren't, get a price quote on rentals before making your final location decision. You may need:

- ☐ Dinnerware (including any available upgrades)
- ☐ Cake cutter and server
- ☐ Chairs (chair covers and tie backs)

- ☐ Tables (reception and cocktail)
- ☐ Linens (tablecloths, napkins, runners)
- ☐ Riser or stage for the DJ/band
- ☐ Plants and trees (to fill a bare space—your florist might take care of these, too)

- Is in-house catering available? Can we bring in our own caterer?
- Can we use our own outside vendors for the florist, DJ, etc., or must we use their staff?
- Does the site have a liquor license? Can we bring in our own alcohol? If so, what types of alcohol will be served, and is there any cap or limit?
- Is ours the only reception scheduled that day? If not, will there be another one during our reception?
- Will we be sharing cocktail hour space or bathrooms with the other guests? Will we be able to hear their music during our reception?
- Will the manager be present for our reception?
- What are the cancellation policies? Is the deposit refundable?
- What's the staff to guest ratio?
- How many hours is the site available? Are there charges if the reception runs over?
- Is there free parking? If there is valet parking, what are the rates and expected gratuities?
- Will there be coatroom and restroom attendants? Servers? Bartenders? What are the charges for each?

☐ before you leave, be sure to have:

- Price list
- Menu, if applicable
- Copy of the floor plan, if available
- Digital photos of the space
- List of references
- All contact information

booking your reception site

Even if you're overjoyed with the space, don't feel rushed to reserve it on the spot. We know the threat of losing the space is going to snip at you, but give yourselves time to compare and contrast prices, notes, and impressions.

☐ call references and ask the following:

- Were you happy with the overall service of the facilities?
- How would you rate the site on a scale of one to ten?

- Were there any problems? How were they resolved?
- Did they accommodate your requests?
- What sort of feedback did you get from your guests about the reception?
- Did the site look as good in pictures as in person?

☐ book the site.

☐ ask for a contract with all your ideas and details, including a sketch of the room, if possible.

☐ location of your wedding (that is, "rooms a and b" or "presidential ballroom")

☐ list of rentals (chairs, tables, linens, centerpieces)

☐ name of person who will be on hand the day of and the name of a substitute

☐ any other agreements you've discussed

RECEPTION SITE CONTRACT POINTS

Confirm that the following is included in your reception site contract:

☐ Your names and contact information
☐ Your event date and time
☐ Reception company's name and contact information
☐ Detailed description of your reception

☐ Cancellation and refund policy
☐ Total cost and an itemized breakdown of what's included (gratuity?)
☐ Deposit amount
☐ Payments to be made, in what form, to whom, and due dates

finalizing reception details

From making floor plan arrangements to deciding if a garter toss is archaic (it is), it's time to pull together the final elements of the day. Unless otherwise specified, provide the final guest count a week before the wedding.

☐ decide on a room diagram.

Your reception site manager should have good ideas based on his or her experience.

- Where will the dance floor go?
- Where will the band or DJ be set up?

- Where will the cake table be set up?
- Where will the escort cards/favors be set up?
- Where will you sit? Your wedding party? Your parents?
- Where will the buffet tables go (if applicable)?
- How many tables can fit, and in what sizes and shapes (square, round, banquet)?

☐ coordinate deliveries to the reception site.

Fill the site in on all the details when it comes to deliveries. And let vendors on the other end know your reception location and exact room location to avoid any confusion.

☐ make timeline decisions.

Decide whether you want to do a bouquet toss, when you want to cut the cake (traditionally, an hour before the end of the reception), and how you want to be announced. Give the timeline to your reception manager so that he will have it on hand the day of. Here's what a basic timeline involves (elements can always be added or taken away to fit with your schedule and style):

- Cocktail hour
- Couple and/or wedding party announcements
- First dance (go to page 161 for ten classic first dance songs)
- Dinner
- Toasts/speeches
- Cake cutting
- Bouquet/garter toss
- Exit
- After party

☐ take care of postwedding details.

- Decide who will take gifts home from the reception.
- Figure out alternative transportation options for those who have had too much to drink.
- Make arrangements to pick up any large décor items (your florist's vases, the rental company's chair covers).

{ your favors }

Favors may be small, but they show your appreciation for your guests and they're the perfect send-off from a great reception. You don't have to spend a ton of money (the average favor costs about one to five dollars per guest); finding fun favors is all about adding a personal touch. Follow these steps:

→ what will we consider in choosing our favors?

- Locale (if it's a wedding at a winery, mini wine bottles or a silver stopper)
- Wedding colors (lemon drops in mini tins for a wedding awash in yellow)
- Season (for a winter wedding, give out mini packets of hot chocolate)
- Your love story (fortune cookies if he proposed with one)
- Travel/honeymoon (luggage tags are a cute idea)
- Your monogram (shortbread cookies frosted with your new monogram)
- Philanthropy (give back with a donation to a charity in each guest's name)
- Eco-consciousness (green ideas like tree saplings or soy candles)

→ how will we personalize our favors?

From monograms to caricatures, putting a personal stamp on your wedding favors is a sure way to get (and keep) guests' attention. Just make sure to mention your names and wedding date.

→ how will we package our favors?

Wrapping is a way to give any favor designer status. Think:

- Handmade paper wrapping
- Simple boxes
- Takeout boxes
- Tiny tin pails
- Slim silver canisters

→ how will we present our favors?

It's all in the presentation. So take some time to figure out where you want guests to pick up their thank-you. A few options:

- At each place setting (a simple wrapped box at each setting is pretty)
- On a favors table near the exit (for guests to grab on their way out the door)
- Passed around (by the waiters on silver trays)
- As centerpieces at each table (set up in the shape of a pyramid or stacked)
- As table numbers or escort cards (a donation card)

chapter 3

The ceremony *is* the wedding, so don't wait until the last minute to plan. There's much more to this event than simply saying "I do": You need an officiant who gels with your specific wishes (civil but spiritual, a mix of religions), a program that artfully guides your guests (explaining the rituals and when guests should stand), and, of course, a dose of aisle style (runners, flowers).

- Know your
  guest count
- Know your
  wedding date
- Know your
  state's mar-
  riage license
  requirements
- Know the mar-
  riage require-
  ments of your
  religion

organizing your ceremony site

You might already know that you're marrying in the house of worship from your childhood, or the church your grandparents and parents were married in. If you already have a place of worship lined up, skip to the officiant section on page 31. If not, this section is for you—we'll focus on finding a secular space for your ceremony. Your reception site is a great place to start (is there an adjacent room?), or try for a site that's completely different and unique.

→ what kind of ceremony do we want?

- Religious
- Civil (secular)

→ what sort of location matches our vision for the ceremony?

- A house of worship
- Indoors in a secular space
- Outdoors

→ who do we want to attend the ceremony?

You should invite your entire guest list, but if you're feeling über-shy, you can consider including just your family. Regardless, your ceremony attendees must be invited to the reception.

☐ call potential sites to make an appointment. but first confirm the following:

- Wedding date availability
- Guest capacity

☐ check out the ceremony sites.

Overall, make sure the style of the site fits with your taste. Picture yourself and all your guests gathered in the space, and decide whether you'll feel comfortable walking down the aisle there. Ask yourselves:
- Does this location fit with our style and tastes?

- How far away is this from our ideal reception space?
- Do we like the acoustics?
- Is there a good spot to take formal pictures?

☐ ask about decorating the space.

- If the space is bigger than we need, can we rope off rows?
- What décor will the site provide (aisle runner, ribbon, other items)? Can we bring in our own décor and flowers?
- Are there any décor restrictions? (Some places don't allow aisle runners, rose petals, or birdseed.)
- Can we take the flowers with us?

☐ find out logistics and if there are any quirky rules.

- Can worshippers from other faiths attend the ceremony?
- Are there any rules regarding photography and videography?
- Are there restrictions on the music that we can have?
- Can we include family members or close friends in the ceremony elements?
- What is the parking situation?
- Is there a bridal suite or room for us to use?
- Will there be any other weddings that day?

☐ ask about the staff.

- Who will we be dealing with the day of?
- Do you provide musicians?
- Can you help choose readings and music?

☐ if you're planning on an outdoor ceremony, there are special considerations. ask:

- What will our backup plan be in case of inclement weather?
- What will the landscape look like at the time of the wedding?
- Will the outdoors potentially affect our or our guests' allergies?
- How will we keep guests cool if it's a hot day, and warm if it's a cold day?
- Will the ground be even enough for chairs and an aisle?

- Will we have access to electrical equipment for microphones and amplifiers?

☐ before you leave the appointment, be sure to have:
- List of included services
- List of policies
- List of references to call if you're having your ceremony at a completely separate venue
- All contact information

☐ book your ceremony site.

Sign the contract and pay any deposits. Make sure your contract includes:

- Your names and contact information
- Ceremony site company name and contact information
- Detailed description of your ceremony
  - ☐ Exact date, time, and location of your ceremony (name of chapel)
  - ☐ List of extras the site will provide (aisle runners, flowers, music)
- Name of person who will be on hand the day of and the name of a substitute
- Any other agreements you've made orally
- Cancellation and refund policy
- Total cost and what's included
- Deposit amount
- Payments to be made, in what form, to whom checks should be made out, and due dates
- All signatures

working with your officiant

This person is crucial. He or she will help set the tone of your ceremony and will work with you to create the perfect words for the day. You need someone whose beliefs coincide with yours, and who is as modern or traditional as you desire (especially if you want to change phrases like *obey* or *man and wife.*) You may have a ready-made ceremony package (your childhood pastor); if not, read on.

☐ find an officiant.

- Start with your house of worship. (Ask if there is anyone available for your wedding date. Or, is there someone they require you to use? Can you bring in outside officiants? What about co-officiating?)
- Ask for recommendations and browse the web for officiants. (You can go the civil, spiritual, or religious route. Go to TheKnot.com/local for reputable officiants in your area.)
- Call up city hall. (Find a justice of the peace, mayor, county clerk, or other government worker who is authorized to perform a marriage ceremony.)
- Consider having a friend or family member perform the service. (Go to TheMonastery.org to find out how someone can be ordained for the day.)

☐ arrange an interview.

At the interview, assess the officiant's personality and open-mindedness. Decide whether this person makes you feel comfortable enough to conduct your ceremony. Ask for an overview of the following:

- How long is your typical ceremony?
- Can we write our own vows or help personalize the ceremony? If so, can you provide guidelines?
- Do you have standard vows if we don't want to write our own?
- Can we include family members in the ceremony?
- For a civil service, can any religious elements be included?

why do we put the ring on our fourth finger?
The Egyptians believed the "vein of love" ran from the heart to the ring finger, so placing the ring on that finger meant eternal love.

☐ find out about any specific marriage requirements.

- Are there any papers to be filled out or filed?
- Do we have to attend premarriage counseling?
- Can another officiant (of another faith or from a different place) take part in the ceremony?
- Will you give a sermon or speech? If so, can we see a copy of what you'll say beforehand?
- Do you permit photography or videography during the ceremony?
- Will you perform the ceremony outside of a house of worship?
- Will you travel within the area?
- Will you conduct the rehearsal?

☐ ask about fees.

Some religious officiants may only require a donation to the house of worship. Others have a set fee.

☐ seal the deal.

You probably don't need a formal contract, but make sure you have something in writing confirming the date of service, contact information, and fees.

planning your ceremony music

Before you make any music decisions, check with the officiant for their guidelines. Some churches won't allow secular music, and some rabbis won't allow Wagner's "Here Comes the Bride" because of the composer's alleged anti-Semitism. Then ask yourselves these questions:

→ how formal do we want our music to be?

- Traditional
- Traditional mixed with some secular
- Completely secular

→ what general genre do we want played?

It doesn't all have to be the same, but it does help to have a little bit of a cohesive sound. So pick a style and then stray from it a little during the processional or, better yet, the recessional.

→ are there any must-play songs for our ceremony?

Think of the songs that have meaning to you—a favorite hymn, the song that was playing in the car on your first date—and incorporate them into the ceremony.

NEW IDEAS

Don't skimp on ceremony music. Instead, infuse your personal style with one of these cool combos.

- Classical (Get a string quartet or vocalist, or go for a flute trio or two guitars.)
- Folk (Think bluegrass band complete with a banjo.)
- Jazz (Hire a jazz group featuring a trumpet, or go for a more muted sax or piano.)

- Reggae (Think steel drum band or electronic guitar, bass, and drums.)
- Country (You could feature a great vocalist and an accompanying guitar.)
- Gospel (Think belt-it-out choir or one single voice.)

is there a good time to marry?
Chinese tradition says that couples should marry on the half hour so that they begin their new life on an upswing—when the hands of the clock are moving up.

greek ceremony tradition
During the Eastern Orthodox crowning tradition, the best man, or *koumbaros*, places one of two ornate crowns on the bride's and groom's heads. The crowns are connected by a ribbon that literally unites the bride and groom for the remainder of the service, symbolically tying them together for the rest of their lives.

→ **what musicians do we want included in our ceremony?**

A few popular choices:

- Organist, pianist
- Vocalist
- Bagpiper
- String quartet
- Harpist

☐ **find potential musicians.**

- Browse local wedding magazines for names of ceremony musicians.
- Check out TheKnot.com/ceremony for names of musicians in your area.
- Go to bridal shows to listen to demos and meet prospective musicians.
- Ask recently married friends or your house of worship for suggestions.
- Seek out local university music department professors for student group recommendations.
- Look through postings on local websites or newspapers.

☐ **check out potential musicians' websites to listen to music samples.**

☐ **call up ones who interest you. ask about availability, fees, and music specifics:**

- Do you have a playlist?
- Are you open to playing things not on this list?
- Can you suggest works that fit with our style?

☐ **if you like their music style, ask about ceremony specifics:**

- Will you attend the rehearsal?
- What will you be wearing at the ceremony?
- Have you performed at our site before?
- How soon before the ceremony will you arrive?
- What equipment do you require? What do we need to provide?

- For an outdoor ceremony, what will you need if it rains? (String players will need to take cover to protect their instruments.)
- If you're ill on the ceremony day, who will be your backup and can we meet him or her?

☐ get everything in writing. even if it's not a formal contract, have your ceremony site draft a document or an e-mail to spell out all the specifics:

- Your names and contact information
- Ceremony musician's name and contact information
- Name of a substitute in case of emergency
- Your wedding date, ceremony site address
- Attire guidelines
- A list of what they will play and when (Also include some B-list songs to play should they need to fill time.)
- Amount of time they are expected to perform
- Fees and overtime rates (Write in a clause that ensures their flexibility should you need them to play longer— during the prelude, for example.)
- Cancellation and refund policy
- Deposit amount due
- Balance and date due

WORDS TO KNOW

When thinking about your ceremony music, consider that there are four general parts to the ceremony.

- Prelude: Also called seating music, it sets the mood for the ceremony as guests enter and are seated. Plan for an hour's worth of music.

- Processional: Played as the wedding party walks down the aisle, the music usually changes for the bride. Choose two songs, or three if you want the mothers to walk to a different tune.

- Recessional: Played as the couple and the wedding party walk back down the aisle, it's usually upbeat and signals that the festivities are about to begin.

- Postlude: After the couple's recessional song, the musicians should continue to play as guests slowly exit the ceremony site. This can be a reprise of some prelude songs.

creating your ceremony

Once you've finalized all the details with your ceremony site and officiant, you'll need to take care of a few more ceremony elements.

☐ decide which rituals to include in the ceremony.

The ceremony is one of the most personal aspects of the wedding—unique to your backgrounds, cultures, and ideals. For a Catholic ceremony, many couples choose to include the ritual of offering roses to the Virgin Mary; for a Jewish wedding, couples usually perform a glass-breaking ritual. Here are some basic ceremony rituals to consider:

- Vow exchange (traditional or original?)
- Ring exchange
- Readings (How many? Who will give them?)
- Unity candle lighting (or wine-sharing ritual)
- Ketubah signing
- Moment of silence
- Offering to ancestors
- Musical performance
- Sermon
- The kiss (Okay, this is kind of an obvious one, but will it be a long, drawn-out smooch? A sweet peck?)

☐ create a ceremony timeline.

Put together an outline of the ceremony and the time each will take.

- Seating
- Prelude
- Processional
- Vows
- Sermon
- Readings
- Rituals
- Special music
- Recessional
- Receiving line

☐ decide where each person will stand during the ceremony.

- When will our families walk in? (Who will escort them? From which entrance?)
- When will our groomsmen walk in? (From which entrance? In what order?)
- When will the groom walk in? (From which entrance?)
- When will our bridesmaids walk in? (From which entrance?)
- When will our ring bearer and flower girl walk in? (From which entrance?)
- When will the bride walk in? (Who will she walk with?)
- Will our wedding party stay standing, or will they sit?
- Will we stay standing, or will we sit?
- In what order will our wedding party exit?
- In what order will our families exit?
- Where will they stand after they exit?
- Who will stand in the receiving line? (In what order?)

☐ gather everything you need for the ceremony.

- Tables, altars, or chairs for the traditional rituals
- Aisle runner
- Pew markers/flowers
- Flowers for the altar/chuppah
- Flowers for the aisle
- Arrangements for the ceremony entrance
- Vows, if personalized
- Programs (See Chapter 8: The Invitations and Stationery.)

☐ decide where your ceremony musicians will set up.

Whether it's on the second level in the choir balcony or outside beneath a large oak tree, figure out where you want your ceremony musicians to play.

☐ get your marriage license.

Check your local clerk's office for all the details. Go to TheKnot.com/license to find marriage license information in your area. Usually, you are required to have the following:

- Birth certificates
- Driver's licenses
- Proof of age
- Proof of citizenship
- Blood tests and doctor's certificates (few states still require this)
- If applicable, proof of divorce or annulment
- A fee (usually $10–$30)
- Witnesses while you sign the license

☐ take care of postwedding details.

- Decide what will happen with ceremony décor. If you use any flower petals or rice for your exit, decide who will clean it up.
- Make sure all arrangements have been made to tip your ceremony site manager and take care of your officiant.

☐ plan out your rehearsal.

Usually the actual rehearsal occurs on the day before the wedding, preceding the rehearsal dinner. Do the following to prepare:

- Decide what time it will take place.
- Tell your officiant.
- Tell your ceremony musicians.
- Tell all the players when to be there.
- Make copies of the ceremony timeline for each person involved.

how did the sides of a church get separated?
Fathers used to offer their daughters as peace offerings to warring tribes, but because of the hostility, the families were placed on opposite sides of the church so the ceremony would take place without bloodshed.

{ your wedding bands }

You'll wear it till, well, you know, so before you commit to a wedding band make sure it's one you'll love now and forever. Plan on buying your bands three to four months before the wedding to make sure they're ready in time for the ceremony. If you're interested in a custom piece or intricate engraving, give yourself more time. Follow these steps:

☐ **browse online for styles that catch your eye.**
Are they simple? Ornate? Covered in diamonds? Go to TheKnot.com/ wedding bands to search ring photos by price or style.

☐ **go to jewelry stores and try on rings.**
Decide if you want matching bands (it's not required). Also, ask if the shop that sold your engagement ring offers a discount if you buy a wedding band there too.

☐ **decide on the type of metal you like.**
- Platinum (It's more expensive than gold, also rarer and very durable)
- White Gold/Gold (It's less expensive than platinum and can be colorful; but it's not as pure as platinum.)

☐ **narrow it down to your favorite rings. Ask yourselves:**
→ How does the band look with the engagement ring? (Many brides choose to wear the rings on separate hands, especially if they're both ornate designs.)
→ Does it include quality marks?
- Make sure bands have two marks inside the shank: the manufacturer's trademark (which proves they stand behind the work); and a quality mark (24K or PLAT). If the ring consists of two or more metals, make sure there is a quality mark for each.
→ Can this ring be personalized or modified?

☐ **size it right.**
To find the size that will weather all the changes, do your final ring fitting when you are calm and your body temperature is normal.

☐ **engrave it.**
Add a special touch. It can be as simple as your wedding date or as sentimental as a favorite saying. Check spelling, and double check the delivery date.

{ chapter 4 }

Wedding food has gone gourmet. From
interactive stations to decadent dessert
buffets, creating the perfect personalized
menu is a top priority—and, in actuality, part
of your overall wedding style. Plus, it's one of
the things guests remember most about your
wedding. That's why making an effort with
your menu and selecting a caterer who can
carry out your culinary vision is a must.

- Know whether
  your site will
  include
  catering
- Know your
  approximate
  guest count
- Know your
  wedding date

envisioning your menu

Your choice of what to serve goes far beyond chicken or beef. From choosing a style of service to finding ways to infuse a menu with some personal flair, many decisions go into making a memorable meal. Ask yourselves these questions to start narrowing down what you want:

→ what meal do we want to serve?

Dinner receptions are the most common, but brunch and lunch receptions are gaining in popularity. Tea, cocktail, and dessert receptions are affordable—and stylish—alternatives.

→ what kind of food do we like?

This is where the personalization comes in. Jot down some of your favorite foods, flavors, and restaurants, and use this list to decide what best captures your palate preferences: Continental cuisine, regional, seasonal, comfort, or ethnic.

→ what type of service do we want?

Consider the style of your wedding. Decide whether a casual buffet, a family-style seated meal, or a formal waiter-served affair would complement your celebration best.

→ how many courses will be served?

The traditional reception meal is a sit-down, four-course meal: appetizer, soup, entrée, and dessert. Additional courses include hors d'oeuvres, salad, fruit and cheese, and pasta.

→ what entrées will we offer?

Standard options include beef, chicken, or seafood. But you could also go for pork, lamb, or pasta. Decide if you want to give guests options.

→ does anyone have any dietary restrictions?

Consider your vegetarian guests and those who keep kosher or halal when mapping out your menu. You may want to look for a caterer who can create a few alternative meals in addition to your main choices.

→ how will food be served at the cocktail hour?

Keep in mind that you'll want to order a mix of cold and hot hors d'oeuvres and that everything you order should be easy to handle. Choices include:

- Passed (staff-served) hors d'oeuvres
- Hors d'oeuvre tables (more casual)
- Food stations (raw bar, crepe table)

→ what kind of dessert will we serve?

Add a little sweet something to the end of your reception meal beyond the wedding cake. Consider:

- **Ethnic treats:** Maybe it's a French croquembouche or a Danish dough ring cake.
- **Miniature bites:** From mini crème brûlées to mini pieces of French toast.
- **Retro favorites:** Serve moon pies and baked Alaska.
- **Seasonal items:** If it's summer, serve lemon granita; if it's winter, serve warm fig pudding.

NEW IDEAS

- Comfort food: Take the formal edge off by serving old-fashioned classics like mac and cheese or curly fries.

- Mini foods: Bigger isn't always better—miniature burgers are sure crowd-pleasers.

- Heavy hors d'oeuvres: Skip the seated meal and opt for more filling appetizers instead.

- A tasting plate: Don't make your guests choose—give them some chicken and beef and fish.

→ how will we serve dessert?

If it's a formal dessert following dinner, have it served plated to each place setting. If things are a little more casual, set up a fun dessert table so your guests can grab a bite as they head onto the dance floor.

→ what type of dishes do we want to use?

Consider china and silver for a formal sit-down dinner, or colored glass dishes for a more laid-back affair.

→ can we bring in our own alcohol? (if not, skip to page 46)

Supplying your own alcohol can be a way to save on your wedding reception expenses. If it's allowed, determine how much of each beverage you will need for each portion of your reception.

STANDARD OPEN BAR AMOUNTS (PER 100 GUESTS FOR FOUR-HOUR RECEPTION):
- Champagne: 18 bottles
- Red wine: 10 bottles
- White wine: 18 bottles
- Beer: 2–3 cases
- Whiskey: 1–2 liters
- Bourbon: 1–2 liters
- Gin: 2 liters
- Scotch: 3 liters
- Rum: 2 liters
- Vodka: 6 liters
- Tequila: 1 liter
- Dry vermouth: 2 bottles
- Sweet vermouth: 2 bottles
- Tonic: 1 case
- Club soda: 1 case
- Cranberry juice: 2 gallons
- Orange juice: 1 gallon
- Grapefruit juice: 1 gallon

FOR A CHAMPAGNE TOAST (PER 100 GUESTS):

- 1½ cases or 18 bottles (assumes 6 glasses per bottle, 1 glass per person)

WINE FOR DINNER (PER 100 GUESTS):

- 4+ cases or 50 bottles (assumes 4–6 glasses per bottle, 2 glasses per person)

☐ **find a liquor discounter or wholesaler. (ask your caterer for referrals or search online.)**

☐ **order and pay for the liquor with your credit card.**

Obtain a receipt of sale that includes an itemized list of all products and amounts, which items will arrive chilled, and the exact delivery date, time, and address.

☐ **make sure you have the bar supplies covered.**

Your bartender should supply tools (shakers, ice tongs) and do the prep work. Your caterer should be in charge of glasses and know of any special requests (martini glasses, champagne flutes).

think a modern-day reception is long?
Colonial wedding dinners were commonly feasts lasting two to three days, depending on how wealthy the family was. The main course was usually served family-style and included entrées like fish, roasted pig, duck, pumpkin casserole, and rye bread.

finding caterers

Preparing food (that actually tastes good) for a large group of people is no easy task, so it's important to entrust your wedding day menu to someone with talent. Follow these steps:

☐ **figure out what services you want your caterer to provide.**

If you decide to go with a caterer that only provides the food, you'll need to make provisions—either with your reception site or with a rental company—to ensure your tables will be set. Will they provide the following?

- Wedding cake (Whether you use your caterer or a baker, check out Chapter 10 for everything you need to know.)
- Bar
- Service/waitstaff
- On-site coordinator
- Rentals

☐ **gather names of local caterers:**

- Use local magazines or TheKnot.com/caterers
- Check with your favorite restaurant to see if they'll cater your affair. If not, ask for other good options.
- Ask your site for their list of preferred caterers or for general recommendations of reputable caterers.
- Contact professional catering organizations (like the International Caterers Association or the National Association of Catering Executives) for referrals.
- Ask recently married friends who were pleased with their caterer.

☐ **browse potential caterers' websites.**

Notice the appearance and presentation of the food. If this caterer provides other items as well (like table linens and dishes), you'll want to take note of those, too. You should also be on the lookout for:

- Sample menus

- Names of sites where they are approved to work
- Awards or professional organization memberships
- Testimonials from recent clients

☐ narrow down your choices.

Look for online reviews of the caterers that are at the top of your list. And if you're bringing outside caterers to your reception site, ask the management if they have worked with any of these caterers and what they thought.

☐ start calling caterers.

Before you make a formal appointment, confirm:

- Caterer's address, phone number, and contact name
- Availablity on your wedding day
- They're within your price range
- They're able to meet your key menu requirements (dietary or otherwise)
- Any specifics about how you envision your wedding day meal (type of service, must-have menu items, number of courses)

WAYS TO SAVE

Serving tuna tartare and filet mignon is obviously going to cost you more than a house salad and chicken Milanese. But there are some other hidden ways to save.

- Limit the number of options. If you want a high-end entrée, your caterer may cut you a deal if you only serve one. This way, there's no need to order extra food that may not be served.

- Stick with the season. The price of many foods, especially fruits and vegetables,

changes month to month. You may reduce catering costs by selecting a menu filled with fresh seasonal produce.

- Serve a signature cocktail. Not only are they chic and fun, but also you'll reduce the number of liquor bottles opened, which is a big savings. (Most caterers charge by the number of bottles that are opened, so if each one of your guests has a hankering for a different type of booze, you're going to open—and be charged for—more bottles.)

interviewing caterers

Taste is important—after all, you want guests to delight in the food—but it isn't everything. When interviewing caterers, you are also trying to determine their experience level and professionalism.

☐ explain your wedding vision.

Use this time to tell the caterer what you foresee for the menu and find out if they will be able to accommodate your requests. Also, bounce ideas off the caterer and allow him to offer suggestions or options you haven't considered. To break the ice, consider asking:

- How many events do you cater each year?
- What was the most unique event and/or menu you created?
- Do you specialize in certain types of food?
- How involved are you in a typical reception? Do you fill wedding coordinator/banquet manager role?

☐ ask for photos and/or sample menus from weddings they've done.

Does the caterer's work match your style and taste? Ask:

- Can we alter your sample menus, or completely customize a menu?
- What do you think would be most appropriate for our wedding style?
- How do you arrange the food on the buffet table(s) and/or on plates? Can we see photos of previous displays?

☐ ask about tastings.

Some caterers will schedule the first interview and tasting on the same day, while others will set up an initial meeting and then follow up with a tasting based on your specific ideas. Either way, you'll want to do a tasting before signing any dotted lines. Some points to consider:

- Are you willing to include a recipe we provide that has some sentimental significance? Can you prepare vegetarian, kosher, or halal meals for some of our guests?

- How far in advance is the food prepared?
- Do you have a printed price list for food selections?
- What are the best menu combinations?
- Is there anything we need to take into consideration given our wedding date or location? Any foods we should avoid?
- While tasting—do we like the balance of food on the plate? Is there too much meat or too many potatoes?
- Do we like the flavor? Is it too overpowering, or too bland?
- Do we like the dishes and the tableware choices, or will we want to order our own?

☐ assess their personality and professionalism.

This is where the interview can get a little tricky. It's not enough for the caterer to have good food—they have to be good at timing and orchestrating the meal as well. When interviewing, start thinking about whether this is someone you'd trust with a big piece of your wedding. Observe the environment they work in and, if you can, talk to some of the staff members. You want to get a good feeling about your caterers—one that says not only can they cook, but they can be trusted, too.

☐ ask about service details.

- Do you work with the same servers regularly?
- How much experience do your servers have?
- What is their attire?
- Who is our main contact? Will this same person oversee the meal service on the day of the wedding?

☐ find out about any other services they provide.

- Do you provide tables, chairs, plates, table linens, silverware, salt and pepper shakers, and more? (Ask to see them to make sure they meet your standards.)
- Are you working any other weddings the same weekend, day, or time as mine?
- Do you handle the setting of all tables? Will you put out my place cards and favors?

roasted pig
anyone?
Traditionally in
Italy, a roasted
baby pig or lamb
was served up to all
the wedding guests
along with *wanda*,
which is fried
dough dusted with
powdered sugar
and shaped into
bow ties.

- Do you have a set wine list, or can we make special requests? How is this list priced? Can we have a wine tasting?
- Is there a corkage fee if we provide our own alcohol? How and when should we get the alcohol to you?
- Do you do wedding cakes? If we bring in an outside baker, will you charge a cake-cutting fee?

☐ collect this information from your caterer before leaving the interview:

- Business card with all the caterer's contact information
- Rough outline of services, including cost per person, menu options, what the fees include, service and presentation style, and less expensive alternatives
- At least two references—these should be previous clients who had a similar number of guests and menu

booking your caterer

Now that you've had the opportunity to meet with and sample the work of a few different caterers, carefully weigh your options. Taste, price, variety of options, wine list, and overall experience should be factors in your final decision.

☐ check references.

Yes, this means actually contacting your vendors' past clients. Here are some important points to cover when talking to references:

- Go over background information: number of guests, venue, menu, etc.
- Find out how satisfied they were with the meal. Was it good, hot, and well presented?
- Ask about the service. Were guests served and tables cleared efficiently?
- Were there any surprises on the final menu or final bill?
- Were there any day-of problems? How did the caterer deal with them?

- Was all the food prepared and served on time?
- Was the caterer pleasant to work with? Did he/she respond quickly to your calls and/or e-mails?

☐ choose a caterer and reserve their services.

☐ send a fax or e-mail to confirm your wedding date and time with the caterer.

Also, give a rough outline of the menu and the number of guests, and be prepared to pay a nonrefundable deposit.

☐ finalize your food and drink menu with the caterer.

Choose which courses you want served, which foods you would like, and which drinks you want served alongside.

☐ request a contract from the caterer.

Make sure all foods and services are itemized on the contract. Keep in mind that you'll need to pay a deposit when you sign the contract.

organizing your menu and catering needs

With a caterer secured, you can now focus on the other fun food and drink details.

☐ research rental companies for items that your caterer and reception site don't provide.

If neither your caterer nor your reception site offers extras like linens and dishes, you'll need to bring in a rental company to supply these goods. Turn to page 21 in Chapter 2: The Reception for a list of what you need.

☐ coordinate delivery and setup between your caterer and reception site.

Give your reception site the name and contact information for your caterer. Make sure your site manager and caterer speak about when the food will arrive and where it will be arranged and stored.

☐ decide when and how the food will be served.

Whether you're having a buffet or a formal sit-down meal, you'll need to come up with a plan for how the food is presented to guests. Here are some things to cover:

● If you're having a buffet, decide where in your reception hall you want the food set up.

CATERER CONTRACT POINTS

Your catering contract isn't complete without all (and yes, we mean all) these points:

● Name and contact information for you and the caterer
● Date, starting time, and length of reception
● Location of reception, including exact address and name of room, if applicable
● Date by which the caterer needs a final head count
● Approximate number of guests
● Staff details: waiter to guest ratio, number of bartenders
● Type of service (cocktails, buffet, tea, dessert, seated meal, etc.)
● If buffet, will you be charged by guest or by plate count?
● Specific menu (you can make alterations later)
● Acceptable food substitutions (in case of unavailability on wedding day)

● Liquor: what kinds and how much (if the caterer is providing)
● Cake: layers, flavors, and ornamentation (if the caterer is providing)—see Chapter 10 for more cake contract details
● Rentals: what's included (tables, linens, dishes, silverware, etc.)
● The name and contact information for the person who will oversee catering on wedding day
● Proof of license and liability insurance
● Cost per person (usually three levels: adult, child, and vendors)
● Extra fees: sales tax, gratuities, bar or corkage fee, rentals, delivery, cake-cutting fee, fees for extra waitstaff, and kitchen fee
● Total estimated cost of service
● Deposit amount
● Balance amount, due date, and preferred method of payment
● Cancellation and refund policy
● Caterer's signature

- If you're having a sit-down dinner, figure out the order in which you want the tables served. (Grandma will not be happy if she's the last served!)
- If you're having cocktails and passed hors d'oeuvres, start thinking about whether you want everything served at the same time or if you'd prefer one type of hors d'oeuvres at a time.

☐ order any extras for the wedding day.

Consider the following:

- Staff meals for your on-site vendors (the band and photographers)
- Snacks in the bridal suite (fruit and cheese are a good idea)
- Boxed lunches for the day of the wedding
- Midnight snack (for you two when the party is over)

☐ decide how you will ask your guests their menu preferences. many couples choose to include it in the invite option with the RSVP.

☐ confirm the menu and get that information to your stationer or calligrapher for the menu cards.

☐ call your caterer to confirm final head count and final payment. (the final amount and preferred form of payment should be included in your contract.)

☐ calculate service tips for the staff if not included in the fee.

- Determine who gets a tip and how the money will be distributed. Tipping is essential.
- Main reception contact: $200–$300
- On-site coordinator: $200–$300
- Waiters and bartenders: $25–$50
- Parking and coat attendants: $1 per guest

{ chapter 5 }

Don't take your guests for granted—after all, they bring the fun to the party. This is why creating the perfect guest list (and taking care of those who've said yes) is essential. The guest list also happens to be one of the most potentially dangerous parts of planning a wedding (as you probably know, the risk of hurt feelings is high). Just remind yourselves and your families that a wedding is not an excuse to bring together every person you've ever known. Instead, focus on the people who matter most now.

• Know your
wedding date

• Know your
budget

• Know the
maximum
capacity of
your location

deciding whom to invite

The trick is to set guidelines. That way, when anyone questions your decision, you'll tactfully explain that you didn't have the space to invite said group (whether it's kids, dates, or coworkers) across the board. Another rule of thumb: Invite 10 percent more guests than your target number since typically between 10 and 20 percent will decline. Before you make your list, ask yourselves these questions:

→ who's paying?

Traditionally, when the bride's parents paid for everything, they would determine the guest list size, as well as the number of people the groom's family could invite. Nowadays, with multiple parties contributing to the wedding fund, it's much more common for the couple to decide the total number of guests to invite and how it will be divided between the bride's parents, the groom's parents, and the couple.

→ what's our budget?

Remember, most reception sites and caterers charge a per-person fee. Dividing your expected reception budget by this flat rate will give you a good estimate of how many people you can invite.

→ what's more important to us: a larger guest list or a specific locale?

If you choose more people, find a venue that will comfortably accommodate them. If location is most important, find out how many people your space can seat and invite accordingly.

→ will we invite coworkers?

In theory, it would be nice to be able to invite the people you spend most of your weekdays with to your nuptials. But because you probably won't have much time to spend with them anyway, and they may not know very many other people at the wedding, this is a good place to start cutting.

Shortcut: TheKnot.com/guests

→ what are our limits on extended family?

If you're worried about hurt feelings, don't be! Remember that your remote third and fourth twice-removed cousins probably feel as indifferent toward you as you do toward them. The same goes for distant friends. And just because someone invited you to their wedding doesn't mean you are obligated to invite them to yours.

→ should we eliminate the "and guest" option?

Another way to trim the guest list is to not give your single friends and family the option of bringing a date. Assure them there will be other singles there and that you won't sit them at a table full of couples. This option doesn't extend to married, engaged, or even well-established couples. And the rules are different for your wedding party—regardless of their marital status, they should always be given the option to bring a date.

→ do we want to invite children?

There are pros and cons to allowing children to attend your wedding—adorable pictures, not-so-adorable outbursts— so it's up to you to decide what will work best at your affair.

finalizing your list and other guest details

Now that you've considered all your options for inviting people, you can get started building a final guest list. Here's how:

☐ decide on your final target guest number and get a final list from each family. collect this information:

- Full name and title(s)
- Spouse name and title(s)
- Address (with zip code)
- Phone number
- E-mail address
- Children's names and ages (if you're inviting them)

☐ put all the information into a spreadsheet so that you're able to sort the names several ways.

☐ keep track of responses.

Once you've sent out your invitations, you'll need to set up a way to manage the replies. Whether you manage your guest list online (go to TheKnot.com/GuestListManager) or on paper, here are some things to track for each guest on the list:

think your list is out of control?
Wedding invitations used to be announced by a town crier—whoever heard the announcement was invited.

- RSVP—attending/not attending?
- How many guests?
- Bringing children?
- Where are they sitting?
- Menu choices?
- Wedding gift received? What was it?
- Thank-you note sent?

☐ reserve individual hotel rooms or block out a group of rooms for out-of-town guests.

☐ create a guest list for events during the wedding weekend.

Decide who's going to be invited to the following:

- Rehearsal dinner (go to page 65 for more info on this night-before fete)
- Welcome dinner (for out-of-towners not invited to rehearsal dinner)
- Postwedding brunch (turn to page 68 for more)

☐ follow up with phone calls to tardy responders.

☐ give the caterer/reception site a final head count.

☐ give the guest list to your calligrapher/stationer for the escort cards, as well as place cards.

creating a seating chart

Decide whether you want to give table assignments. If it's a buffet for thirty, it's probably not necessary. But if it's a sit-down for one hundred guests or more, you'll want to make sure everyone has a chair. Start your chart at least a week before the wedding day. Here's how to get started:

☐ create a seating spreadsheet.

Use columns to categorize all invitees by relationship, and then separate the lists into tables.

- Bride's friend
- Bride's family
- Groom's friend
- Groom's family

☐ draw it out.

Get a room diagram from your reception site or draw circles (for tables) on a big sheet of paper.

☐ decide who's going to sit where.

Use the diagram to write in guests' names at each table (make sure you know how many guests fit at a table). Or, write every guest's name on a Post-it and place accordingly. Take these tips into consideration when placing people:

- Put an even number of guests at each table (because people tend to pair off in conversation, and you don't want anyone to be left out).
- Put partiers near the dance floor—they'll get things started right.
- Don't put your single guests at a table full of couples.
- Mix and match your friends with friends of your (soon-to-be) spouse.
- If certain family members don't get along, don't seat them together—your wedding isn't the time to play peacemaker.
- Put people with similar interests and of similar ages together.

☐ make head-table seating decisions.

Whether you're having a traditional head table or sitting among your guests, decide who will sit at the table with you. Your choices for a head table might include the following:

- Just the two of you (at a sweetheart table)
- You two and your bridal party
- You two and your parents and family

☐ decide if you're going to have place cards in addition to escort cards.

Escort cards let guests know which table they are sitting at and let them decide which seat to take; place cards assign a specific seat to each guest table. Decide who is going to distribute the place cards, if you're having them.

☐ give the final seating chart to your reception site manager and/or your wedding planner.

planning guest activities

Weekend weddings have become the norm. What does this mean for you? You should take care of your guests from the moment they arrive to the moment they say good-bye. This doesn't mean that you need to spend every second together (or even pay for their free-time activities), but you should suggest ways they can stay amused. Ask yourselves:

→ who will be in charge of coordinating details?

Consider asking a friend or close relative to be the point person for pre- and postwedding activities, rather than taking it all on yourselves.

→ what times do we need to plan activities for?

• Daytime activities one to two days before the wedding
• Dinner the night before (during the rehearsal dinner)
• Between the ceremony and reception (if there's a long lag time)

→ what types of activities should we plan?

It can be a casual get-together, like a barbecue lunch or a margarita happy hour. Or, you could just congregate at a local restaurant. And consider transportation options for guests (see Chapter 14 for ideas). Some other activities you might want to plan:

- Outdoor sports
- Golf outing
- Spa outing
- Beach day
- Baseball game
- City tour
- Museums and private tours

→ how will we let guests know about the activities?

There's no need for formal invitations here, just add an insert to your invitation, or put an information packet together in the welcome bags. Also, be sure to post the information and contact numbers on your wedding web page.

☐ put together welcome bags.

Thank travel-weary guests by leaving them a nice surprise in their hotel room. Think a basket of fresh fruit, tin of local chocolates, or a bottle of wine. Here are some tips:

- Find the right container. It could be anything from a beach bag to a brown paper bag.
- Decide what treats you want to include in the welcome bag. The perfect combo is a bottle of water, a piece of fruit, something sweet, and something savory.
- Include essential information
  - ☐ Names of other guests staying in the hotel
  - ☐ Phone numbers of the families of the bride and groom
  - ☐ Nearby hot spots to check out
  - ☐ Copy of the wedding itinerary
  - ☐ Local brochures and sightseeing maps
  - ☐ A personal thank-you note
- Deliver the bags. Appoint a person or make a time yourself to deliver the welcome bags. This may mean coordinating with the hotel to get into the rooms early, or coordinating their delivery to the welcome dinner.

the
other
parties

{chapter 6}

There's not just the one (huge) celebration to
think about—kick off your engagement with a
cocktail party; throw a rehearsal dinner to
remember; extend the wedding-night
celebrations with an after-party; and send your
guests off with a postwedding brunch. And,
lucky for you, the other prewedding events
(bridal shower, bachelor/bachelorette party)
fall primarily to your wedding party
(remember to thank them for this!). Those
are covered in Chapter 7, but in the meantime,
here's what you need to take care of.

planning your engagement party

• Know your
  approximate
  guest count

• Know your
  wedding date

• Book your
  reception and
  ceremony site

It's the big kick-off to this exciting year (or so) and completely optional. Tradition has it that the bride's parents host the initial gathering, but the groom's parents can then throw their own party, both sets can come together to host the fete, or your wedding party can plan an informal gathering. Here's what you need to do.

☐ decide on a date.

This won't be a surprise party, so give the hosts a few days to choose from, no more than three months after the proposal.

☐ share your guest list.

Know that everyone who is invited to the engagement party should ultimately be invited to the wedding. That said, if you're having a small wedding and want to throw an extravagant engagement party, go for it. Just be sure to let people know that the wedding will be small so no feelings will be hurt when guests aren't invited to the wedding. And, to dispel sentiments that this party's purpose is to receive gifts, include a nice note in the invitation that requests no presents.

☐ register!

It's smart to register for some items to give guests an idea of what fits your style. Turn to Chapter 15 for all the details on registering.

☐ prepare to toast.

You don't need to rehearse anything. Just know that you should raise a glass to your hosts and guests, thanking them all for coming. Get used to it—you'll be toasting them again at most prewedding events.

☐ keep track of gifts.

Create a guest-list spreadsheet to keep track of which guests give you what. That way, when the gifts start arriving, you'll be able to send thank-you notes out right away.

planning the rehearsal dinner

Throwing a rehearsal dinner—a post-practice party on the eve of the wedding— is a great way to unwind, bond, and kick off the festivities (many claim it's the best part of a wedding weekend). Here's how to organize yours.

☐ **agree on who's hosting the event.**

Traditionally, the groom's family organizes and pays for this party. The bride's family, you and your mate, or a combo can play the host role.

☐ **decide whom to invite.**

The guest list should include the wedding party and your immediate family. You might also choose to invite your out-of-town guests, or the entire guest list.

☐ **choose when to throw the party.**

Typically, it's the night before the wedding. Another option is to have an intimate rehearsal dinner two nights before the wedding, then an all-inclusive welcome party the night before.

☐ **set the formality and decide what kind of "dinner" you want.**

- just hors d'oeuvres and drinks
- a light dinner
- full-service dinner

☐ **find a space.**

Restaurants are the natural choice, but a boat, beach, or art gallery can work too. Consider these questions:

- Does it have to be within walking distance from the hotels? From the rehearsal/ceremony site?
- Are there places around town that hold special meaning to us? (Where you got engaged? Your favorite hangout?)
- Does the site need to have any special amenities? (AV equipment for slideshows, outdoor space, DJ)

☐ **check out the space.**

Once you've found a couple of places that spark your interest, make an appointment to find out the essential info.

☐ **book a space.**

Make sure you sign a contract or have some sort of agreement in writing regarding the detailed description of your rehearsal dinner.

☐ **decide on décor.**

Figure out whether you'll bring in flowers, use place cards, or need any extras.

☐ **make timeline decisions.**

A basic timeline may involve the following:
- rehearsal at the ceremony site
- cocktail hour
- dinner
- slideshow
- toasts/speeches
- dancing/entertainment
- good-byes

NEW IDEAS: REHEARSAL DINNER

The rehearsal dinner should have its own personality apart from the wedding—add a little balance to the weekend with a laid-back barbecue or something that reflects the locale, like a clambake. Think of cuisine twists like:

- Tapas
- English tea party
- Cuban
- Grill out
- Clambake
- Chinese banquet
- Comfort food

throwing an after-party

An after-party is more than just an extension of your wedding day—it's a great way to show off more of your wedding style with surprising details and personal touches. Here's how to get the party started.

☐ choose a space.

Consider a local pub, a close friend's or family member's home, a motel, or a smaller room at your reception venue.

☐ estimate your final head count.

You should invite everyone who came to the reception. That said, you can probably make a general guest-count estimate based on your crowd.

☐ spread the word.

Official invites are not necessary. Instead, print the after-party info on a separate card to be sent with your wedding invitations, post it on your wedding website, or simply have your wedding party spread the word.

☐ set the schedule.

How late do you want the party to go? This is completely up to you. But keep in mind that many bars close around 2 or 3 a.m. A good rule of thumb is two to four hours, depending on the time your reception ends.

☐ set the style.

Choose a theme that's different from your reception. Had a casual outdoor wedding? Treat guests to a Latin-themed after-party, complete with salsa music and cigars, and a mojito bar.

☐ provide a midnight snack.

It's important that you provide some bites for your guests. Consider varying the menu from your reception. A great idea: mini burgers, french fries, and milkshakes.

☐ take care of the bar.

If you've rented out a reception space, it's expected that you'll continue the open bar. If you've booked a space at a bar or lounge, it's a generous and appropriate gesture. But if it's a less formal let's-hit-this-pub type of event, it's not necessary.

hosting the postwedding brunch

At the end of the weekend, a brunch is a great way to wind down and exchange final good-byes. You can take this chance to thank your guests and spend a bit more time with loved ones who've traveled far to partake in the celebration.

☐ decide who is hosting the event.

Traditionally, the bride's parents, but it's a nice gesture to pay for it yourselves.

☐ decide on a location.

The location depends entirely on your personal tastes. It could be as casual as your or your parents' home, as convenient as a spare room in the guests' hotel, or as formal as an upscale brunch restaurant or hotel.

☐ make a guest list.

The brunch is usually for the couples' families and any wedding guests who are still in town, but feel free to include attendants and friends.

☐ send invites.

Insert a card inside the wedding invitations for the guests you want to invite. Or, send out a separate mailing. The cards can be as formal or as casual as the brunch itself.

☐ set the menu.

It's up to you whether you want a catered affair or a simple, homemade pancake brunch with friends and family. Some ideas:

- The standard brunch (omelets, French toast, waffles, pancakes, scones, bagels, coffee, and juices)
- Cocktail brunch (add ancho chili paste to French toast or add orange blossom mascarpone to fresh crepes; for cocktails, serve mimosas and bloody Marys)

the
wedding
party

{ chapter 7 }

They'll be there to zip your dress and decorate
your getaway car; to roast you and toast you;
to grin and bear it when you make them wear
salmon taffeta dresses and ties (please don't).
They're your bridesmaids and groomsmen—
your VIP team. You'll need to know how to
choose them, dress them, and ensure they
have a great time.

BEFORE
YOU BEGIN

• Know your
  approximate
  guest count
• Know your
  wedding
  location

choosing your attendants

Choosing the bridal party can be one of the toughest (read: political) decisions you make. Beyond your bridesmaids and groomsmen, keep in mind that there are other roles to fill. You can appoint ushers, candle lighters, a guest book person, and even junior bridesmaids to take part in your day. Scan these questions, and the selection process will be a breeze.

→ how many people do we want in our wedding party?

One guideline is to have one groomsman and one bridesmaid for every fifty guests. Also, a large wedding party traditionally signifies a more formal wedding.

→ do we care if the bridal party is even?

It's okay to have five on one side and three on the other. What matters is that you each have your closest friends near you.

→ will we include family in our wedding party?

Decide whether you want to include siblings, cousins, or other close family members in your bridal party, or if you'd rather keep it friends only.

→ will we include out-of-town friends in our wedding party?

Think twice about asking friends who live far away or who have extremely hectic schedules if you expect them to be involved in all the festivities.

→ do we want friends of the opposite sex to stand up for us?

If your best friend is of the opposite sex, there's no reason why he can't be a bridesman and she a groomswoman. Decide together the best way to include those closest to you both.

→ do we want children in our wedding party?

A flower girl is usually aged three to eight and a ring bearer is usually aged four to eight. Depending on the child's maturity level, you can go younger or slightly older.

☐ choose the winners (just kidding).

But really, finalize your list together—you both have to be happy with who's standing up for you. Call or talk to them in person (no e-mails or voicemails) to ask them to be in your wedding party.

☐ dole out other special roles.

Have too many good friends? Keep in mind that there are plenty of other roles good friends can play in your wedding if they don't make the cut—do a reading, hand out programs, or perform a song.

groomsmen duties

What's expected of these guys? Read up and pass the info on.

- Attend and organize bachelor party
- Rent or buy his own formalwear
- Help (when possible) with prewedding tasks like transportation
- Arrive early at the ceremony location to assist with any last-minute setup
- Act as ushers if you haven't already assigned others the role
- Play host to guests at the wedding and prewedding parties
- Make sure that the gifts from the wedding are transported properly
- Decorate the getaway car

best man duties

- Organize the bachelor party with the other groomsmen
- Drive the groom to the ceremony
- Hold the bride's ring until it's needed in the ceremony
- Witness and sign the wedding certificate
- Might be in charge of giving payments to all appropriate vendors
- Give a toast at the reception

maid of honor duties

- Attend important shopping trips with the bride such as gown fittings
- Take charge of planning a bridal shower with the other bridesmaids
- Arrange the bride's veil and gown at the altar
- Hold the groom's ring until it's needed at the ceremony
- Hold the bride's bouquet while she says her vows
- Witness and sign the marriage certificate
- Might stand in the receiving line
- Might give a toast at the reception
- Help the bride change clothes after the reception and take care of the gown

bridesmaid duties

Your bridesmaids will ask you a million times what they can do to help. Here are some good ideas:

- Attend and organize the bachelorette party
- Attend and put together the bridal shower
- Usually will pay for her own wedding attire
- Assist the bride in prewedding shopping
- Help (when possible) with prewedding tasks like addressing invitations, making shower favors
- Arrive early at the ceremony to help the bride dress
- Play hostess to guests at the wedding and prewedding parties

flower girl duties

- Walk down the aisle just before the maid of honor, scattering rose petals or holding flowers along the bridal path behind the ring bearer—sometimes she precedes the bride.
- Traditionally, she totes a basket full of petals, but alternatives include a pomander or a single bloom.

ring bearer duties

- The ring bearer walks down the aisle just before the flower girl, carrying a pillow with two rings tied to it—the rings are usually fakes.

wedding party parties

Let's be honest, one of the best parts about weddings is all the parties leading up to it—the showers, bachelor parties, and luncheons. Even if you're not planning the shower or the bachelor party, you'll need to help gather guest lists and dates, and give your input when it comes to overall style. Here's how to be prepared!

→ the bridal shower

Traditionally, a shower is a party for the bride and her closest female relatives and friends, where she is "showered" with love, good wishes, and gifts. Often the bridesmaids host the bridal shower and the maid of honor puts it all together. But it doesn't have to be this way. If a coworker wants to put together an at-work shower, or your mom wants to throw one, that's fine too.

☐ decide on a date.

It's often a surprise to the bride, but it should take place two months or so before the wedding day.

where did bridal showers begin?

In Holland, when a bride's father didn't approve of the fiancé, he wouldn't give her a proper dowry. The bride's friends would then shower her with gifts so that she would have a dowry and could marry the man of her choosing.

☐ share your vision for the day.

Though you have no control over this party, let your brides-maids know whether you'd prefer a lunch or dinner, as well as how formal you'd like for it to be (laid-back barbecue or swanky cocktail lounge). Also, let them know how you feel about guys being involved in the shower.

☐ give your guest list.

Everyone invited to the shower should also be invited to the wedding. Create a list of friends and family you'd like to attend the shower. If it's a couple shower, make it a coed guest list.

☐ register.

You will have already filled out your registry for your engagement party, but just take a moment to make sure that you've covered all your bases. This is the time guests are really going to be looking at it.

☐ make a plan for the presents.

You'll probably be opening gifts at your shower, so make sure you have a plan in place to get those gifts back home. Decide who will help you carry them and where you're going to store them once they make it home.

☐ thank your hosts.

Send out a formal thank-you note to the host or hosts of the party, thanking them for throwing you a shower. You can even send them a special gift like a flower arrangement.

→ bridesmaid luncheon

The bridesmaid luncheon is a chance for the bride to thank her bridesmaids for all of their help leading up to her wedding day. Usually, it's a laid-back event, hosted by the bride, where they can chat, reminisce, and relax before the chaos begins.

☐ decide on a date.

The bridesmaid luncheon usually takes place a day or two before the wedding, when all the out-of-town attendants have arrived.

☐ create a guest list.

Traditionally all the female attendants in the wedding party are invited (bridesmaids and flower girls). But it's up to you. If you want your mom or grandmother to be there, include them.

☐ decide where to host the luncheon.

It could be lunch, brunch, dinner, or light hors d'oeuvres—really whatever fits your style. And it can be as formal or casual as you like, whether you want to go completely over-the-top with a served meal at a restaurant, or a more laid-back gathering at your home.

→ bachelorette/bachelor party

Though this party is intended as a night on the town for the soon-to-be marrieds, it's really the bridesmaids and the groomsmen who tend to have the most fun—after all, they're the ones planning and hosting the event. Traditionally, the bridesmaids and maid of honor plan the bachelorette party; and the groomsmen and the best man plan the bachelor party. Then again, if a close friend or relative wants to plan one for you, that's okay too. Here's what you need to do:

☐ share your no-way list.

Yes, they're planning the party, but if there's anything that you're really opposed to (say, strippers), you should let your pals know before the planning really gets under way.

what was the role of the best man?

In England, the best man would keep a sword in his hand during the wedding, acting as a body-guard to the bride and groom. Usually the best swords-man was chosen as the best man.

☐ choose a date.

The bachelor and bachelorette parties generally take place two to four weeks before the wedding day. Try not to have it the week of the wedding; you'll need time to recover.

☐ give a guest list to the host.

Anyone invited to the bachelor or bachelorette parties should be invited to the wedding as well. And it's best to keep the group under twenty people. Then again, if Mom or Dad wants to join the group for dinner and a few drinks early in the evening, that's okay, too. Just make sure there are PG-rated events planned that they can be a part of.

NEW IDEAS: BACHELORETTE PARTY

- Choose a destination that makes you feel like a kid again (like an amusement park)
- Indulge in a spa day or weekend
- Soak up the sun somewhere nice in the middle of winter
- Plan an old-fashioned sleepover (no boys allowed!)
- Go shopping—rent out a boutique and try on outfits for your night on the town
- Try something new—take a cooking, improv, or a wine-tasting class

NEW IDEAS: BACHELOR PARTY

- Eat like kings. Feast on a dinner of steaks and bottles of scotch all around
- Rent a yacht and hire a DJ for the night
- Hit the links and take a guys-only golf getaway
- Hit the beach—sit back, soak in the sun, and let the drinks come to you
- Be daredevils—go bungee jumping or cliff diving
- Try something new—learn to fish, hit a baseball, brew beer

browsing for bridesmaid dresses

Now that you've chosen your attendants, you'll need to find the right attire for them. Get their input: It pays to have happy bridesmaids. Want some ideas before you hit the shops? Go to TheKnot.com/bridesmaids for fabulous bridesmaid dress inspirations. And ask these questions about your bridesmaid dresses:

→ what does my gown look like?

Look for styles that complement your gown. If you're planning to don a ball gown, your bridesmaids will look too casual in teeny mini dresses.

→ what is our color scheme?

If you've chosen colors that don't translate into bridesmaid dresses, choose a more wearable yet complementary hue. For a sea foam green wedding, choose cool blue dresses.

→ how formal is our wedding?

Formal and semiformal weddings call for long, ballerina-length, or tea-length dresses. Bridesmaid dresses at informal or daytime weddings can be shorter.

→ what are my bridesmaids' body types?

Consider choosing the color and then allowing them to choose the style. They'll be happiest in a style that they feel comfortable in. (If you're into the uniformity thing, choose a simple and universally flattering silhouette like an A-line.)

→ do I want my maid of honor to wear something different?

You might want to distinguish your honor lady in some way or another. Do so by giving her a different hairstyle, dress look, shoes, or bouquet.

shopping for bridesmaid dresses

☐ **find a shop.**

Gather names of local and national dress shops from friends, bridal websites, and bridal shows. If there's a designer you like, see where her dresses are carried.

☐ **check out prospective dress shop websites.**

For complete convenience, see which ones offer online services for your out-of-town attendants.

☐ **call shops to make appointments.**

You'll want to make two trips. First, with one or two bridesmaids, and maybe Mom, to do the overall scouting. Then, once you've narrowed down the selections, bring all the bridesmaids in town.

☐ **start shopping.**

Bring photos of dresses you've seen online or in magazines that you absolutely love. And ask:

- Can you recommend styles for a group with different sizes/body types?
- How do you handle orders and fittings for out-of-town bridesmaids?
- Do you ship dresses?
- How far in advance do we need to order?
- Do you do in-house alterations?
- How much is shipping? Will packages be insured?

☐ **before you leave, be sure to have:**

- Prices and style numbers of your and your bridesmaids' favorite dresses
- Policy outline
- All contact information

☐ **decide on the dress.**

Get together with your bridesmaids (or chat via e-mail) to discuss which dresses you like best. Then, have the maid of honor call or go online to order the dresses (she'll have to have all the girls' measurements first).

☐ decide who will pick up their dresses and who will have them shipped.

☐ make sure to request a letter of agreement with the receipt. it should include the following contract points:

- Your name and contact infomation
- Salesperson name and contact infomation
- Your wedding date
- A detailed description of bridesmaid dresses
- Sizes or measurements the salon is sending to the manufacturer
- Written alterations list and estimate
- Approximate delivery date
- Number of fittings included in the price (if any)
- Amount of money owed on the dresses
- Amount of deposit and date paid
- Balance and due date
- Cancellation and refund policy

☐ have them pay with a credit card (your bridesmaids are typically responsible for the cost).

If something goes wrong with the dresses, you'll want to be able to dispute any payments.

☐ select attire for child attendants, or give their parents guidelines.

how far back does the bachelor party tradition go?
Stag parties were first held by ancient Spartan soldiers, who kissed their bachelor days good-bye with a raucous party.

researching formalwear

And what about the guys? Ask yourselves these questions to determine their corresponding look:

→ **how formal is our wedding?**

Formal and semiformal weddings call for suits or tuxes. More casual and laid-back weddings could include less formal options.

→ **what is our color scheme?**

You may want to consider bringing your wedding colors into your and your groomsmen's attire. That could mean red pocket squares or vests with a hint of green.

→ **do you want groomsmen to wear something that they own or rent the same styles?**

Consider allowing the groomsmen to save some money wearing their own suits or tuxes if they have them.

→ **what extras do we want for the guys?**

Consider adding a few extras like cuff links or pocket squares to personalize and give uniformity. Hint: Buy them their accessories and have them monogrammed as your gift to them.

finding a formalwear shop

Once you know a little better what you're looking for, you can begin looking for a formalwear shop.

☐ **gather names of local and national rental shops based on what you're looking for.**

- Use local magazines and TheKnot.com/local to find area rental shops.
- Ask friends who have recently married or were recently groomsmen for names.

☐ check out prospective formalwear shops' websites and narrow down your choices.

To make it easier on yourselves and your groomsmen, you may want to use a national vendor that offers online services for out-of-town attendants.

☐ call formalwear stores to make appointments.

☐ bring the following with you:

- Formalwear shop address and phone number
- Photos of tuxes or suits you've seen online or in magazines that you like
- Your groomsmen or best man, or at least their sizes.

☐ if renting, ask:

- How far in advance do we need to reserve our rentals?
- What are the different styles you offer?
- How old is the formalwear you rent?
- Before we order, will we be able to see the actual suit that we'll be renting?
- How do fittings and alterations work?
- When will it be ready?
- What are the fees involved?

NEW FORMALWEAR IDEAS

- Wear a subtly different jacket from the rest of the groomsmen. (Put yourself in a one-button jacket and have the groomsmen sport a three-button version.)
- Wear a tie or bow tie that's a different color from the gang's ties.

(Have the groomsmen match the bridesmaids and you can match your bride.)
- Get a unique boutonniere to single yourself out. (Have your florist add an extra accent to yours, or wear a completely different flower.)

☐ if buying, ask:

- How far in advance do I need to order?
- Are alterations extra?
- How many fittings will I need?
- Do I need to bring anything to the fittings?
- Do you sell shoes and accessories?
- When will it be ready to pick up?

☐ before you leave, be sure to have the following:

- Prices of the styles you like
- Policy outline
- All contact information

renting or buying the formalwear

Don't make any hasty decisions. Take some time away from the shop to compare notes on your options.

☐ choose a store and a style to go with, and call or go online to place your order.

☐ make sure to request a letter of agreement with the receipt, and that it includes the following contract points:

- Your name and contact info
- Salesperson name and contact info
- Your wedding date
- A detailed description of the formalwear
- Size or specific measurements
- Alterations list and estimate
- Number of fittings included in the price (if any)
- Amount of money owed on the formalwear
- Amount of deposit and date paid
- Balance and due date
- Cancellation and refund policy

☐ pay with a credit card (typically the groomsmen's responsibility).

If something goes wrong, you or the groomsmen will be able to dispute a payment made with a credit card.

finalizing attendant details

☐ obtain swatches of the groomsmen ties and bridesmaid dresses to show your florist.

☐ select shoes and accessories for the attendants, or give them loose guidelines (black heels, no long necklaces).

☐ follow up with attendants to make sure they have their attire and accessories ready for the wedding day.

☐ decide where everyone will get dressed the day of.

☐ decide where everyone will stay and find out when they are arriving.

☐ decide who will do the hair and makeup for your bridesmaids and who will pay for it (for more, turn to Chapter 12: The Gown).

☐ decide in what order everyone will stand at the ceremony and how each person will walk in.

☐ decide what gifts you want to get for your attendants and buy them. you should also buy a token of appreciation for your parents.

The best scenario is to give these gifts out the day before the wedding in an intimate setting, so as to not make it awkward for those not receiving presents.

the
invitations
and stationery

chapter 8

As the main introduction to your event, the wedding invitation—and the design and wording you choose—sets the stage for your wedding style and guides guests on what to wear and how formal an event to expect. It's a small piece of paper that makes a big impact. But the big decision here is: Are you going to go catalog or custom (that is, choose from a set portfolio or design your own)? Both offer amazing options that can establish your theme with a splash. Let's get started finding the perfect invites and more.

creating your stationery

● Know your
guest count

● Know your
wedding date,
time, and
location

● Know your
wedding style

With so many stores and brands to choose from, let alone books of designs to flip through, choosing the perfect stationery is no easy task. First, think about exactly what you want to order and how you want it to look.

☐ nail down the formality.

- A traditional wedding usually calls for a more classic invitation, with white paper, engraved printing, and a formal lettering style.
- A modern wedding might favor a mix of formal wording with colored paper or a themed motif.

☐ get an idea of what's out there.

Browse invitation designers' websites (found through bride, vendor, or TheKnot.com recommendations), or head to a local stationery store that carries wedding invitation albums. Browse the sites, or flip through the portfolios to get a sense of your style options and what comes in the set.

☐ consider how much you want to personalize.

Do you have a signature motif to use? Or a completely new shape or font you want to try? Many couples customize with their monogram or wedding colors, too.

☐ decide if you want to order from a set portfolio or create your own.

The major difference is price and design freedom. Big stationers like Crane's offer a wealth of options, but your customization choices may be limited. A custom stationer or designer will work with you on an existing style, or create your invitation from scratch.

→ what exactly do we want to order?

Decide which ones you want, and which to forgo.

- Save-the-date cards (includes your names and the date and location of your wedding)

Shortcut: TheKnot.com/invitations

- Invitations (could include several pieces)

  - ☐ Outer envelope
  - ☐ Inner envelope
  - ☐ Reply cards (sent with your invitations with a self-addressed stamped enveloped)
  - ☐ Reception cards (to tell guests where it will take place)

- Rehearsal dinner invitations
- Printed maps
- Travel and hotel information
- Parking and transportation guides
- Ceremony programs (see page 96 for more)
- Menu cards for each setting or table
- Place cards
- Escort cards (direct guests to their tables)
- Table cards (distinguish tables from one another)
- Thank-you cards
- Favor tags

→ what's our budget?

Plan to spend about 3 percent of your overall budget on your stationery needs.

☐ decide whose names will go on the invitation.

Typically the hosts and the bride and groom are listed. But it's not so simple; there are often complicated relationships involved. See the sidebar on page 91 for wording suggestions.

NEW IDEAS

Want to make a chic statement? Choose one of these invitation trends:

- Perforated reply cards (think 2-in-1 designs)
- Locale-inspired designs (beach elements, mountain motifs, lighthouses)
- Hot colors (orange, brown, and coral)
- Designer envelopes (they get an upgrade with colors and patterns)
- 3-D embellishments (charms, appliqués, and more)
- Bellybands (a paper or ribbon wrapped around the invitation)

☐ decide how you want to phrase the invitation.

The wording of your invitation depends on the formality of your wedding. If it's a laid-back beach wedding, you can swap phrases like "request the honor of your presence" for "to join in the celebration."

☐ figure out dress code information.

If you have a strict dress code, it may be best to include that information right on the invitation. But if there aren't any strict guidelines, you may be able to rely on the formality of the invitation and your wedding website. Some useful phrases:

- Black tie
- Black-tie optional
- Jackets required
- Beach formal
- Flip-flops required

☐ figure out how much information you need to convey.

Will you send invitations to other gatherings in the same mailing as the formal invitation? Or will you send them separately or just direct guests to your wedding website?

WORDS TO KNOW

- Engraving: The most formal of printing methods, through which the letters appear slightly raised.

- Thermography: Probably the most popular—it's less expensive than engraving. The text is slightly shiny and the back of the invitation remains smooth, without an impression.

- Letterpress: A nice alternative to engraving, but more expensive. The images and typeface appear precise—

individually "stamped" into the paper—and very rich in color.

- Offset: A nice choice if you want to save money, use textured paper, or several different ink colors—with engraving and embossing, you're usually limited to just one.

- Embossing: This technique forms letters and images with a raised relief surface, imparting added dimension to the invitation's design. Blind embossing is the same process with no colored ink.

If one set of parents is hosting, list their names at the top

MR. AND MRS. JOHN L. SMITH
REQUEST THE HONOR OF YOUR PRESENCE
AT THE MARRIAGE OF THEIR DAUGHTER
MARY ANN
TO
EDWARD MALCOLM JONES

If both sets of parents are hosting jointly, you should list both on separate lines, with the bride's parents' names first.

MR. AND MRS. JOHN L. SMITH AND
MR. AND MRS. MARK FRANKLIN JONES
REQUEST THE HONOR OF YOUR PRESENCE
AT THE MARRIAGE OF THEIR CHILDREN
MARY ANN SMITH
TO
EDWARD MALCOLM JONES

If the bride's parents are hosting, but you'd like to honor the groom's parents by including them on the invitation, you simply make the point of noting their relationship to the groom under his name.

MR. AND MRS. JOHN L. SMITH
REQUEST THE HONOR OF YOUR PRESENCE
AT THE MARRIAGE OF THEIR DAUGHTER
MARY ANN
TO
EDWARD MALCOLM JONES
SON OF
MR. AND MRS. MARK FRANKLIN JONES

If everyone is pitching in, the invitations should begin with the marrying couple's names (bride's first) and follow with "together with their parents" before parents' names and the request line.

MISS MARY ANN SMITH
AND
MR. EDWARD MALCOLM JONES
TOGETHER WITH THEIR PARENTS
MR. AND MRS. JOHN L. SMITH
AND
MR. AND MRS. MARK FRANKLIN JONES
REQUEST THE HONOR OF YOUR PRESENCE
AT THEIR MARRIAGE

If the couple is hosting the event, the greeting skips the host line and begins with the request line.

THE PLEASURE OF YOUR COMPANY
IS REQUESTED AT THE MARRIAGE OF
MISS MARY ANN SMITH
TO MR. EDWARD MALCOLM JONES

Or, more casual wording:

MARY ANN SMITH &
EDWARD MALCOM JONES
INVITE YOU TO SHARE IN THEIR
WEDDING CELEBRATION

For information on including stepparents, widowed parents, and more, go to TheKnot.com/invitations.

why is there
an inner
envelope?
Mail used to be car-
ried on horseback,
and the envelope
would often arrive
in bad shape.
Hence, the inner
envelope was
designed as the for-
mal envelope.

☐ decide who will receive RSVPs.

This is the name that will be printed on the reply-card
envelope. The general guideline is that the person hosting
the wedding should receive the RSVPs.

☐ look at printing options.

Do you want raised letters? A stamped look? Or something
that's simple and inexpensive? See our sidebar on page 90
for information on the different methods.

ordering your stationery

Once you have an idea of what you want your invitation to
look like and say—and who's going to print it—make some
final decisions and place the order early. Save-the-dates
should be sent eight months before the wedding; invitations should go out eight weeks before the wedding day.

☐ ask about customization.

- What are our options regarding different pieces for our
  invitations?
- What are our typeface options?
- Can we see samples of different printing techniques,
  paper styles, and type styles?
- Do you have a specialty?

☐ ask about pricing and delivery information.

- What is the price structure?
- When would we need to place an order?
- When would the invitations be ready?
- Do you address envelopes? If so, how do you do this?
- Will we be able to see a proof before any pieces are
  printed?
- What is the payment policy?
- What is the cancellation policy?

☐ double-check your invitation information.

You will likely see a proof, but it pays to make sure everyone's name is spelled right and the date and time are accurate. We've heard of too many careless mishaps.

☐ buy stamps that suit your wedding style.

The post office has tons of choices from the designated wedding stamp to beaches and birds. Or, go to TheKnot.com/shop for customized postage options where you can upload your own photo to use.

☐ set up an RSVP tracking system.

Before you send out any invitations, set up a spreadsheet (if you haven't already) with all your guests' names. That way, you can easily keep track of who's coming when the RSVPs start rolling in. Also use this spreadsheet to mark off who gave you what gifts, and make thank-you note writing a breeze.

☐ order thank-you notes early.

Wedding gifts begin pouring in three months before the wedding. The rule: Gifts received before the wedding demand a thank-you within two weeks of their arrival; after the wedding, within a month of your return from the honeymoon. Some tips for getting them out the door:

- Have two sets of stationery. For shower gifts and pre-wedding presents, you shouldn't use note cards with your new name or new monogram.
- Equip yourself with pens that you like to write with.
- Set up a designated writing area at home. Make sure it's a comfortable place, not too far from the kitchen or bathroom, with a TV or radio nearby.
- Keep your guest list on hand and when gifts come in, write what they gave you next to their name to stay completely organized.

☐ stuff and send wedding invitations.

If you have time, bring your invitations to the post office and ask for them to be hand cancelled (which means that a postal worker hand stamps each envelope with the postmark). Otherwise, they may become damaged or bent if they are run through the machine.

extra considerations

→ do we want a calligrapher? (see next page)

→ do we want to announce our engagement?

Typically listed in your local newspaper, an announcement is usually submitted by the couple's family (but it's completely acceptable for you to announce it yourselves). An announcement usually includes the following:

- Your names
- Parents' names
- Career details
- Places of residence
- Educational credentials
- Wedding date or month (if known)

→ do we want a wedding web page?

A web page is the perfect way to keep guests up-to-date on all the wedding weekend details. Go to TheKnot.com or

WedORama.com and build your own. Consider including the following info on your page:

- How you met
- The proposal story
- Your wedding date
- Ceremony and reception location
- Hotel information
- Travel information
- Registry links
- Photos of the two of you
- List of the wedding party
- An online guest book

hiring a calligrapher

Calligraphers are best found through recent bride recommendations or sources like TheKnot.com/local. Your dealings with the calligrapher should be pretty low-key—you don't even have to use someone in your town. It's all about finding someone whose specific style you like, sending them the items to be calligraphed and a triple-checked spreadsheet, and making sure the work comes in on time (whether by hand delivery or mail). Here's how to get it done:

☐ check out his portfolio.

An experienced calligrapher should have samples of the types of styles they can do (formal, classic, gothic, and so on).

CALLIGRAPHER CONTRACT POINTS

- Calligraphy style selected
- Ink color
- All items ordered (outer envelopes, menu cards, etc.) that will be calligraphed
- Pricing
- Additional charges (extra lines, colored ink)
- Policy for mistakes or late-stage additions
- Detail of how each item will be calligraphed (format for envelopes)

- Guest list date due to calligrapher from couple
- Number of extra envelopes required and date due to calligrapher from couple
- Arrangements for pickup and delivery
- Method of payment and terms
- Sales tax or delivery charges
- Completion date
- Total amount due and any deposit amounts paid

☐ choose which style best suits your stationery.

Torn between two? Show the calligrapher your invitation and ask for a font sample before you make a decision. Maybe he can match the font on the invitation to the envelopes.

☐ review the sample.

The key to good calligraphy has always been consistency: Shape, stroke, weight, spacing, and rhythm are all factors in letter perfection. So be sure to survey as many samples of lettering designs from each calligrapher as possible.

☐ decide what you want calligraphed.

- Outer envelopes
- Inner envelopes
- Place cards
- Escort cards
- Table cards
- Favor tags
- Menu cards
- The invitation

☐ ask about final logistics.

- What is the turnaround time?
- Do you charge per piece or per job?
- Are you willing to stamp, seal, and stuff envelopes?
- Will you need extra envelopes?
- Will you redo mistakes free of charge?

☐ sign a contract.

your ceremony programs

The more involved guests feel in your wedding, the more likely they are to enjoy themselves. This is where a ceremony program comes in.

☐ decide whether you'll have your ceremony programs professionally printed, or if you'll put them together yourselves.

☐ figure out what you want to put in your ceremony programs.

Standard information includes:

* Your names
* The date
* The location
* An outline of the ceremony
* Titles of readings and songs
* Name of officiant
* Names of wedding party members and their relation to the couple
* Names of others involved in the ceremony (readers, soloists, and so on)

☐ extras to consider adding:

* Dedications and thanks
* Remembrance of loved ones who have passed away
* Words to readings, songs, or vows
* Foreign translations
* Explanations of any cultural or religious traditions
* Favorite poem or quote
* Your wedding motif
* A current or heirloom photograph

☐ decide how formal you want your ceremony programs to be.

☐ decide what format you'll print your ceremony programs in.

If it's a summer affair, you might consider having your programs double as fans.

☐ designate someone to pass out the programs.

the flowers and décor

{ chapter 9 }

Nothing short of the bride herself makes wedding guests catch their breath and think "beautiful" as much as your wedding day flowers. They help set the mood (traditional roses or edgy orchids), enhance a color scheme, and even carry the entire theme. Talk about pressure. If the sheer number of options is threatening to throw you into floral overload, never fear. Just take it step by step.

- Know your ceremony and reception location(s)
- Know your wedding colors
- Know your number of attendants
- Know your wedding party attire

determining your floral style

Look for pictures of floral designs that you find pleasing. Browse magazines and books, and look online at The Knot.com/flowers for extensive photo galleries of bouquets, centerpieces, boutonnieres, and ceremony flowers. Ask yourselves the following questions:

→ what's our budget?

About 8 percent of your total budget should go to your wedding flowers. But if the décor is your top priority, bump that up and try to cut corners in another area.

→ what style do we want our flowers to convey?

A modern style will call for geometric arrangements or smooth, clean-lined flowers like calla lilies. A romantic style will lead to lush blooms, such as peonies or roses. An earthy style will include loose just-picked arrangements and organic elements like berries.

→ what are our favorite flowers?

You might want to look to your family (pay tribute to your Asian background with culturally significant peonies; or ask your mother or grandmother what flowers they used at their weddings).

→ what colors do we want?

Keep the following in mind to work with your color scheme:

- Colors at the reception site (drapes, carpet, walls)
- Linens on the tables
- Your bridesmaid dresses

→ do we have any allergies?

You don't want to sneeze your way up the aisle, so make sure the blooms you're considering don't bother you. Ask your bridesmaids if they have any specific allergies too.

Shortcut: TheKnot.com/flowers

→ what's in season?

Though you can pretty much import any flower any time of the year, it's more economical to stick with seasonal blooms.

- Fall: Calla lily
- Spring: Sweet pea
- Summer: Hydrangea
- Winter: Amaryllis

finding florists

Not all florists are the same. Some are event designers who will help conceive the overall look of the day—chairs, chargers, and centerpieces included; and others are craftspersons, who will bring your specific floral needs—bouquets, altar arrangements, and more—to life. Here's how to get started finding a florist right for you:

☐ find out whether your site has an in-house florist.

☐ gather names of local florists and event designers.

- Use local magazines and TheKnot.com/local.
- Ask your reception site manager for suggestions of florists they have worked with before.
- Ask friends who have recently been married—and were pleased with their flowers—for the names of their florists.

BEST FLOWERS BY COLOR

Red	Yellow	Purple	Green
• Anemone	• Mum	• Sweet pea	• Cymbidium
• Dahlia	• Sunflower	• Iris	orchid
			• Button Mum
Pink	**White**	**Blue**	
• Peony	• Lily	• Hydrangea	**Orange**
• Rose	• Stephanotis	• Veronica	• Zinnia
			• Tiger lily

☐ check out prospective florists' websites.

Look for photos of florists' most recent work. Notice whether the designs share a look—this is probably the style they are most experienced with, so make sure it is one you like. Additional information you should look for:

- Names of sites with whom they have a relationship
- Awards
- Membership in professional associations (such as the Society of American Florists)
- Testimonials from recent clients

☐ call two to three florists to make an appointment.

Ask your planner or reception site manager if they have strong feelings about the florists on your list of potentials. But first confirm the following:

- Wedding date availability. Many floral designers limit the number of weddings they will work in a weekend.
- Appropriateness, pricewise. Ask the typical price range and/or the cost of their average table décor or centerpiece.
- Customization capabilities. If you are looking for something unique, confirm that your florist is willing to create an original design.

☐ prepare for your first meeting.

Have ready:

- Your budget (at least some general guidelines)
- Number of attendants needing flowers
- Number of reception tables (for centerpieces)
- Style requirements: colors, favorite flowers
- Photos of floral arrangements you like
- Swatches or photos of your wedding colors and bridesmaid dresses (to make sure bridesmaid bouquets don't clash with the dresses)

☐ visit the florist in person.

Some have storefronts in which to hold meetings, and others will meet with you right in their studio. To break the ice, you could ask:

- How long have you been a florist?
- How many weddings do you do a year?
- What was the most unique arrangement you've made?

☐ check out the florist's work.

Ask for photos of any events the florist has done at your location, so you'll be able to see what worked size- and colorwise. Look to make sure his style suits your taste. (If you are looking for minimal and all of his designs are over-the-top, he's not the perfect fit.) Also, ask:

- What styles do you have to choose from? Can we alter them?
- Can we completely customize an arrangement?
- What types of flowers do you like to work with?
- If you find photos you like, and it's a big studio: Is the same florist available to work on my bouquet?
- Do you offer rental items? Some florists have their own vases and other decorative items. If not, you may have to contact a rental agency.

☐ express your ideas.

Voice any vision you have for the tables or décor. Your ideas should be met with enthusiasm, and your florist should be able to build on your ideas. This is a creative process and you should feel inspired by them. Ask:

- Will you look at pictures we've found to help explain what we want?
- What do you think would be appropriate for our [insert style keywords] wedding?
- What flowers will be in season on our wedding date?
- What flowers should we avoid because of our date?

☐ ask about business details.

- How big is the staff?
- How many people will work on our wedding?
- How many weddings do you do a weekend?
- Where do you get your flowers?
- When are floral arrangements made?
- How are arrangements stored?

why a boutonniere? In medieval times, a knight wore a flower in his lady's colors as a profession of his love for her.

- Do you handle all delivery and setup?
- Do you preserve bouquets after the wedding?

☐ decide whether you would like them to work up a formal proposal for you.

If so, you should review the proposal and go over a few main factors. Consider the following when working with your florist:

- Your budget
- Any specific flowers you want to use
- The colors you're using
- The arrangements you want (see the list on page 107)

BOUQUET SHAPES

- **Posy** (smaller than a nosegay, perfect for brides with smaller hands, or a bridesmaid bouquet)

- **Nosegay** (approximately 16–18 inches in diameter, a densely packed mound of flowers that works best with compact blooms)

- **Round** (generally larger than a nosegay, consists of large flowers that are loosely arranged)

- **Hand-tied** (a bunch of blooms that are casually tied together with ribbon and have a just-picked natural look)

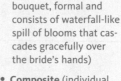

- **Cascade** (or a "shower" bouquet, formal and consists of waterfall-like spill of blooms that cascades gracefully over the bride's hands)

- **Composite** (individual petals from flowers are wired together on one single stem)

- **Pageant** (or a "presentation bouquet," a bunch of long-stemmed flowers cradled in the bride's arms)

- **Pomander** (small and compact bloom-covered ball, suspended from a ribbon worn around the wrist—perfect for a flower girl)

booking your florist

Don't feel pressured to sign on the dotted line right away. Give yourself time to compare and contrast prices, impressions, and proposals.

☐ **call references and ask:**

- Did you approach the florist with specific ideas and suggestions, or did they help you choose your style and flowers?
- How willing were they to work with your suggestions and photos?
- Were the flowers delivered on time and in good condition?
- Did they decorate the church and reception hall?
- Did they work to fix any problems?
- Did the flowers come out as you expected?
- Did you have any problems with your florist?
- How would you rate your overall experience?
- Was your final cost what you expected?

☐ **choose a florist and call to express your desire to book them.**

☐ **refine the proposal and go over all details with your florist.**

The proposal typically acts as your contract and should include:

- Your names and contact information (address, phone, e-mail)
- Your event date, time, location, and phone number
- Vendor's company name and contact information (address, phone, e-mail)
- Name of florist to contact on your wedding day
- An itemized list of all arrangements, including exact names, colors, and amounts
- Flower alternatives
- Unacceptable substitutions
- Other items the florist will supply
- Any needed rentals

- Bouquet and boutonniere delivery place and time (Aim to have these delivered before the photographer arrives so they are available for prewedding photos.)
- Ceremony delivery location and setup time
- Reception delivery location and setup time
- Deposit amount and due date
- Payments to be made, in what form, and dates due
- Balance amount and due date
- Total cost (including tax)
- Cancellation and refund policy
- All signatures

☐ send in the signed proposal with your deposit.

☐ If your florist hasn't worked in your site before, make sure they arrange a site visit.

finalizing wedding day details

Since your florist will buy the flowers for your wedding the day before or day of, you do have time to change your mind a *bit*. What you cannot do is unexpectedly decide to go from an English garden feel to a dramatic monochromatic look. But, you can say that you'd rather swap dahlias for daffodils. Then, once you have finalized all your arrangements with your florist, you need to attend to all flower-related details from delivery to display.

☐ confirm all delivery details with the florist (times, locations).

☐ decide whether you'll toss your bouquet.

If so, you probably want to get a separate, and smaller, toss bouquet. Also, decide where you'll toss it from and who will bring it to you when it's time to do so.

☐ decide which arrangements will be moved from the church to the reception site, and who will make them.

☐ decide whether you'll donate your arrangements, or they'll be given away to your guests.

Keep in mind that elderly care facilities and hospitals greatly appreciate flowers.

☐ decide whether you want to preserve your bouquet and who will do it.

☐ determine what elements need to be picked up from the reception site and given back to the florist or rental company (vases, aisle runner) and arrange for someone to do that.

☐ arrange for final payment and confirm the following:

- Amount: Unless modifications have been made, the final payment amount should be in your contract.
- Payment: Will she accept a check, credit card, or only cash? Who will give payment to the driver upon delivery? Unless the florist herself brings the flowers, a tip to the driver is appropriate.

FLORAL DÉCOR AND ARRANGEMENTS

- Rehearsal dinner centerpieces
- Bridal bouquet
- Toss bouquet
- Bridesmaid bouquets
- Boutonnieres
- Mother corsages
- Grandmother flowers
- Flower girl bouquet
- Additional corsages
- Tossing petals
- Altar arrangements
- Chuppah or wedding canopy

- Ceremony entryway arrangements
- Pew/chair arrangements
- Aisle runner, flowers
- Cocktail hour arrangements
- Reception centerpieces
- Custom linens
- Head table arrangement
- Escort card table arrangement
- Cake topper décor
- Plants or other fillers
- Entry area arrangements

{ chapter 10 }

The wedding cake is so much more than a
sweet treat—it's the exclamation point on
your wedding day. When guests gather around
to watch you cut the cake, the look of the
dessert and how you choose to carry out the
tradition (please, no face smashing!) will
serve as the ultimate unique stamp on your
memorable day.

• Choose your
reception
location

• Hire your
caterer

• Know your
approximate
guest count

determining your cake style

First, you need to have a sense of what you want in a wedding cake. Look through photos either online (TheKnot.com/cakes has hundreds of images) or in wedding books and magazines. While you're browsing, ask yourselves some questions:

→ do we want to go classic or creative, or somewhere in between?

The classic wedding cake is round, white, and usually accented with a floral motif. Or you could go for something modern, such as:

• A colorful cake to match your wedding colors
• A chocolate cake
• Cupcakes or individual mini wedding cakes
• Table cakes (smaller wedding cakes created to serve the 8–10 guests at a table)
• Comfort food cake (a cake studded with Oreos or other favorite foods from childhood)
• A thematic cake (decorated with shells to reflect a beach theme; or fashioned to look like the pyramids to pay homage to a proposal in Egypt)
• Strawberry shortcake, cheesecake, pie, tarts, or other cake alternatives
• Cultural cake (a French croquembouche or a Danish marzipan ring cake)

→ what shapes do we like?

Three classic, stacked round tiers or a tall, towering five-tiered cake in a mix of shapes? How many guests you have to serve will also play into this decision. Don't forget to consider your reception space: If your cake will be displayed in a towering room, taller or extra tiers may suit the surroundings; a space with low ceilings will require a more petite cake.

→ what size cake do we need?

The general rule (and depending on the size of the tiers) is that three tiers serves 50 to 100 guests. So for 150 guests, you'll likely need four tiers or more. If you're serving your cake with sorbet or ice cream, or alongside a dessert bar, you can plan to order a little less cake. Serving sizes (based on round cake tiers):

    8 inches: serves 12–16
    9 inches: serves 16–22
    10 inches: serves 23–34
    12 inches: serves 36–48
    14 inches: serves 47–66

→ what decorative details fit our wedding style?

Even the most minimal of wedding cakes needs some form of decoration to help your wedding style. Your options include:

- **Sugar flowers** (Is there a flower that has a particular meaning to you? Sugar artists can create almost any bloom.)
- **Fresh fruit** (For a fall wedding, use crisp apples; and for a summer wedding, opt for tasty strawberries.)
- **A graphic motif** (Use your monogram, polka dots, or an element from your invitation.)
- **Patterns** (Incorporate a lace pattern from the bridal gown, or latticework to match a garden theme.)
- **Thematic details** (Seashells can complement your beach setting, or use pinecones for your mountaintop ceremony.)
- **Cultural emblems** (Perhaps a double happiness character would be nice if you're Chinese.)

→ do we have a favorite flavor?

If you decide to opt for a special flavor, like ime, you will want to find a baker who specializes in that particular flavor.

→ do we have any ingredient restrictions?

If one of you is allergic to key ingredients like nuts or eggs, or your families have certain restrictions (kosher, vegan, halal; wheat-free), you'll need to find a specialty baker who can fulfill your request. Some bakers also work with all organic ingredients.

→ what's our cake budget?

Cakes can cost from $400 to $8,000 and up; start with 5 percent of your overall budget and know these pricing pointers:

● Per slice cost: Professional cake bakers price their cakes per slice or per serving (anywhere from $4 to $25).
● Complexity affects cost: The more pure the ingredients, the more complicated the structure, and the more ornate the decoration, the more expensive a cake will be.

→ do we want a groom's cake?

Originally a Southern tradition, a groom's cake is a smaller companion cake that was typically cut and sent home with guests. Groom's cakes are often made of chocolate and are designed to reflect a passion of the groom's. Some things to consider:

● Alma mater team mascot
● Favorite sport (a golf course, basketball court)
● Favorite flavor (from red velvet to peanut butter)
● Alternative ideas (forget the cake idea and serve up his favorite sweet, such as Twinkies or doughnuts)

finding bakers

Baking, decorating, and delivering a wedding cake is a unique skill. Unless you are having a very small casual wedding, you will want to work with an experienced wedding cake baker. Here's how to get started choosing a pro:

☐ find out whether outside bakers are allowed in your location.

Some sites will allow outside cakes, but only from their approved vendors. Others will allow you to bring in any cake. If you do bring in an outside cake, most will charge you a cutting fee—priced per slice (usually about $1)—to have their staff cut and serve your cake.

☐ determine who will be responsible for creating
your cake.

Depending on whether you are able to use an outside
baker, you have four options:

- Reception site: At a standard site, you will probably have
  a set selection of cakes to choose from. At a top-tier
  hotel, the pastry chef may even be skilled in the craft of
  wedding cakes and be able to provide unique options.
- Caterer: The same vendor that caters your reception
  may also produce delicious cakes. Your design choices
  may be limited if elaborate cakes aren't their specialty.
- Cake designer: An independent baker who specializes in
  sophisticated ingredients, unique workmanship, and
  detailed decorative techniques—perfect if you're looking for an over-the-top presentation.
- Bakery: You may have limited design or flavor choices,
  but many bakeries have a recognized specialty such as
  multilayered Italian wedding cakes, carrot cake, or
  fruitcake.

☐ gather names of local cake bakers.

- Use local magazines and listings at TheKnot.com/local
  to find the names of bakers in your area who specialize
  in wedding cakes.
- Ask your caterer for suggestions of wedding cake designers with whom they have worked before.
- Ask friends who have recently married—and were
  pleased with their cake—for the name of their baker.

☐ check out prospective cake vendors' websites.

Look for photos of bakers' most recent work. Notice
whether the cake designs share a look—this is probably the
style they are most experienced in, so make sure it is one
you love.

why a
wedding cake?

In ancient Rome,
the ceremony
would end with
breaking a wheat or
barley cake over
the bride's head as
a symbol of good
fortune.

☐ call two to three bakers to make an appointment.
but first confirm the following:

- Wedding date availability. Many cake designers have a limit on the number of cakes they can or will produce in a weekend.
- Appropriateness, pricewise. Ask their typical price range and/or the cost of the average wedding cake they create.
- Customization capabilities. If you are looking for a custom cake, confirm that your baker can create an original design with you.
- Tastings. Will you be able to taste particular cakes?

☐ prepare for your meeting/tasting.

Bring the following with you to the interview:

- Bakers' address and phone number, just in case
- Your budget (at least some general guidelines)
- Photos of cakes, your décor, your gown (anything you've collected to express your wedding style)

WORDS TO KNOW

- **Buttercream:** A smooth, creamy icing that stays soft so it's easy to cut through. It can be colored or flavored and used to cover, fill, or decorate a cake.

- **Fondant:** A sweet, elastic icing made of sugar, corn syrup, and gelatin that's rolled out with a rolling pin and draped over a cake for a clean, smooth finish.

- **Ganache:** A sweet, rich chocolate that's denser than mousse but not as thick as fudge, it's used to cover or fill a cake.

- **Marzipan:** A paste made from ground almonds, sugar, and egg whites rolled in sheets to create a smooth finish. It

can also be used to create lifelike fruit and other garnishes.

- **Royal icing:** A sweet, thick icing made from egg whites and confectionary sugar, usually used for piping, flowers, and borders.

- **Whipped cream:** Heavy cream whipped to stiff peaks, good for fillings.

- **Gum paste:** Sugar, cornstarch, and gelatin combine to mold realistic-looking fruits, flowers, and other garnishes.

- **Molded chocolate:** Malleable chocolate or white chocolate that can be melted and reshaped into garnishes or flattened to cover a cake.

☐ at your first meeting, kick things off by asking about his or her experience.

- How long have you been a wedding cake designer?
- How many cakes do you make a year?
- What was the most unique cake you've ever made?

☐ ask to see a portfolio or sample cakes.

Overall, you are looking to make sure her style suits your taste. If you see a photo you like, check to see whether the same staff members that created it still work there. You can also ask:

- Do you have set styles to choose from? Can we alter them?
- Can we completely customize a cake?
- What do you think would be appropriate for our [insert style keywords] wedding?
- Are the decorative elements edible?
- Do you custom design your own decorative elements (flowers, shells) or are they purchased?
- Will you work with my wedding colors? What do you like to use as a style reference (invitations, photo of gown)?
- Can I use real flowers as decoration? They should offer to work directly with your florist if this is your preference.

☐ taste a piece.

The other focus of the meeting is to taste the product. You should be offered multiple cake flavors and fillings to taste—either in the form of slices, squares, or mini cakes. Sample cakes at room temperature to be sure flavors will hold up even if the cake is on display all day. Ask:

- What ingredients do you use? (The best bakers use fresh ingredients and make their batter from scratch, not a mix.)
- Can you provide a list of cake flavors and fillings? Are any a specialty?
- What are the best combinations? Can I alternate flavors by layer?
- How far in advance are cakes prepared? (Three days in advance is normal and no more than two weeks.)

- Are there any special considerations I need to address given my wedding date or location? (If your wedding will be outdoors in the summer, your baker should have concerns and special suggestions about refrigeration, or avoid certain fillings and frostings.)

☐ express your ideas.

Voice your ideas about your cake design and see how the baker responds—your ideas should be met with enthusiasm. That said, some ideas (a cake tilted like the Leaning Tower of Pisa) may be unrealistic, and you need to respect your baker's knowledge of cake design.

☐ judge their personality and professionalism.

Decide whether you generally like and trust this person enough to give them your business. Ask about business details:

- How many people will work on my cake? (Sometimes there is a separate baker and designer.)
- How are cakes priced? Can you provide a price list?
- Are there any extra labor costs involved?
- Can you work inside my budget? (Tell them how much you have to work with. If your budget is below their range, ask if they have creative solutions to suit your budget.)
- Do you deliver? Do you set it up? (Also ask if there is a delivery fee involved.)
- How many wedding cakes do you handle per weekend? On my wedding weekend?
- Do you have a state health department license? (Don't work with anyone who does not.)
- Can you provide a list of references?
- What is your normal process if I decide to proceed with you? (Will they provide a proposal? A contract? A sketch of your cake or sample decorations for a more unique concept? At what point do they need a final count?)
- Whom do I contact to take the next step?
- Can I communicate with you via e-mail? (Get her e-mail address.)

☐ before you leave, be sure to have:

- Price list
- Flavor list
- List of references
- All contact information

booking your baker

Don't feel pressured to book your baker on the spot. Calling references is important. Also, give yourself time to compare and contrast prices, impressions, and notes.

☐ call references. ask the following:

- Can you e-mail me a photo of your cake? (A good way to confirm the look of the final product.)
- How well did the baker interpret your ideas?
- Was the final cake exactly what you wanted?
- How did the cake taste?
- How many meetings did you have?
- Did he coordinate with other vendors (caterer, florist, reception site)?
- Was the cake delivered intact and on time?
- Was she nice to work with? Did the baker respond quickly to your calls or e-mails?
- Were there any problems? How did the baker deal with them?
- How would you rate your overall experience with your baker?

☐ choose a baker.

Call immediately to express your desire to move forward.

☐ get a contract.

Have your baker write up a contract for you with all of your ideas. It should include a sketch of the cake you're thinking of.

☐ send in your contract.

You'll want to tell them what you think of the sketch and possibly meet with them to discuss any major changes. You'll also usually put down half of the total cost at this time.

CAKE CONTRACT POINTS

Confirm that all of the following information is included in your cake contract:

* Your names and contact information (address, phone, and e-mail)
* Your event date, time, location, and phone number
* Baker's company name and contact information (address, phone, and e-mail)
* Detailed description of the cake you have agreed upon:
  ☐ Cake flavor
  ☐ Fillings
  ☐ Number of servings
  ☐ Number of tiers
  ☐ Tier shape(s)
  ☐ Icing type
  ☐ Decorations
  ☐ Topper
* Cost of cake (price per slice)

* Number of slices (this may be adjusted later if guest count changes)
* Delivery and setup fees (including how and when cake will be delivered)
* Location for delivery (Be exact on how both the name and address of your reception site is noted. Confirm with your site if there is a separate entrance for deliveries.)
* Any related items (e.g., cake stand or cake server) being delivered and rental fees, if any.
* Additional vendor information (florist, caterer, photographer, etc.) if necessary
* Total cost, including delivery
* Deposit amount
* Payments to be made, in what form, and dates due
* To whom checks should be made out
* Cancellation and refund policy
* All signatures

finalizing the cake details

Your cake can't show up without a proper place, right? It's the showstopper of the wedding, so you'll need to create a stylish cake table. Here's a list of details to finalize:

☐ order cake accessories.

* **Cake topper:** If you plan to purchase one online or have one custom-made, make sure to order at least two months prior to your wedding date.
* **Cake serving set:** The knife and server are often a keepsake from the day.

- **Toasting glasses:** A matching set of glasses used for the toast with your guests.
- **Cake boxes:** For guests to take home slices of groom's cake or leftover cake.
- **Cake table decorations:** Items such as votive candles and cake stand.

☐ decide where and how the cake will be displayed.

- **Location:** You'll want your cake to be visible throughout the reception, so ask your catering manager where the cake table works best in your space.
- **Table shape:** An appropriate table (consider a round table for a round cake and a square table for a square one) will need to be rented or supplied by your site.
- **Linens and floral:** Work with your florist or event designer to create the perfect surroundings for your cake. Will there be a canopy over your cake table? Pin-spot lighting?
- **Photos or other personal effects:** Surrounding the cake with your parents' wedding pictures is a nice personal touch.

☐ coordinate delivery with your reception site.

- Inform your site of your cake baker.
- Coordinate delivery. Many sites have particular rules about deliveries. Make sure your site manager and cake baker speak.
- Arrange assembly and storage. Your baker should be in contact with your site or caterer to arrange to have the appropriate space available to assemble and, if needed, refrigerate the wedding cake. Make sure to confirm this conversation has happened.
- Decide whether you're serving a side dish with your cake (raspberry sorbet cups with a sprig of mint or a rich, chocolate truffle), and arrange this with your caterer.

☐ make decisions about the cake cutting.

- When will you cut the cake? Will it be forty-five minutes before the end of the reception? Or right after dinner plates are cleared? (Make sure this time is noted on your timeline. See page 24)
- How will it be announced? Will the bandleader or your DJ make an announcement?
- Will you have a toast? (The cake cutting is a good time for the bride and groom and best man and maid of honor to make their final toast of thanks to their guests.)
- Will there be music? (If you want a song to play while you're cutting the cake, let your DJ or bandleader know. See page 159)
- Which layer will you cut? (It's typical to cut into the bottom layer. Ask your cake baker for suggestions.)
- How will you feed each other? (Will you do dainty bites with a fork or use your hands to feed each other?)
- Who will be served first? (It is customary to serve the bride and groom and wedding party first. However, in Chinese culture it is a tradition to serve slices to the parents before the cake is served to guests.)

☐ arrange for final payment and confirm the following:

- Payment: Will he accept check, credit card, or only cash? And who will give payment to the driver upon delivery? Unless the baker herself brings the cake, a tip to the driver is appropriate.

☐ take care of postwedding details.

- Top layer: Tell your caterer or reception hall if you plan to save the top layer so that they can pack it up for you. (Ask them to wrap it in several layers of plastic and then place it in a crush-proof container.)
- Designate someone like your mom to take the top tier home and freeze it for you.
- Determine what elements need to be picked up from the cake table after the reception (serving set, photos, heirloom topper), and arrange for someone to do that.

The Flavor Report

When you go to your tasting, note what you like—write
down your favorite flavor combinations, as well as any cake
colors and styles that catch your eye.

the
photography
and
videography

{ chapter 11 }

What remains after all the hard work of planning a wedding? It's the many memories and hopefully an incredible album and video. Find a photographer and videographer whose style you like—whether it be formal portraits, photojournalistic, or both. Here's how to get started finding your photo and video pros.

BEFORE
YOU BEGIN

• Know your
  wedding date
• Know your
  ceremony and
  reception
  location

determining your style

Browse magazines and photographers' websites to get a good idea of what you like and what you are looking for in a photographer (soft lighting, edgy angles, campy portraits). There is a range from traditional to more modern documentary approaches to both photo and video. And ask yourselves these important questions:

➜ what style of photography do we want?

- Traditional portraits (posed family group photos)
- Purely photojournalistic (action shots of the day's events)
- A blend of portraits and photojournalistic shots

➜ what events/moments do we want to cover?

- Engagement photos
- Rehearsal dinner
- Wedding day
- Other events (engagement party, bridesmaid lunch, postwedding brunch)
- Your love story (a collection of the two of you)
- Prewedding interviews (bridesmaids, groomsmen, family)

➜ do we want black-and-white shots, color photographs, or both?

➜ what's our budget?

About 12 percent of your overall budget should be allotted to your photography and videography.

finding photographers and videographers

Some companies may offer both photo and video services, but don't feel obligated to order them together. Many photographers operate entirely independently of videographers. Finding talented photographers and videographers to capture one of your most important days is no easy task.

☐ gather names of potential photographers and videographers.

- Browse local and national wedding magazines for names and styles that catch your eye.
- Use TheKnot.com/local to search for photographers in your area.
- Bridal shows can be a good place to look because you can meet local photographers and videographers in an informal environment
- Ask recently married friends or family members for suggestions on photographers.
- Expand outside the wedding realm: Ask artistic friends or acquaintances for referrals to photographers who shoot weddings on the side.

☐ look at potential photographers' websites. notice the overall quality and style of their work. when looking at their photos, assess the following:

- The way each moment is captured (What does the first dance shot look like?)
- Framing of each shot (Does it seem well-composed to you?)
- Special effects (Do you like the way he incorporates effects into the shots?)
- Many photographers are blogging on their websites, where they'll post both photos from weddings and other places as well. These blogs are a great way to see a photographer's work, and a way to get to know their interests outside of wedding photography.

☐ narrow down your choices.

Informally research reviews of no more than three photographers or videographers. Ask your other vendors whether they feel strongly about any of your potentials.

☐ start making appointments for interviews. before you do, confirm:

- Wedding date availability
- Fee is appropriate for your budget
- List of services

interviewing photographers

Not every photographer will have a studio in which to meet you. You may have to meet in a coffee shop if the photographer is independent of a large company. When you meet, you should evaluate the photographer's work, but more importantly, their personality. You will spend your entire wedding day with this person, and they will be present for some of the most intimate moments of your life!

☐ have these with you for the interview:

- Photographer's address and phone number, for reference
- Your budget
- The specifics (style you're seeking, shots you love)
- The locations you want the photographer to shoot

☐ look at sample albums.

Ask to see a complete wedding album, not just a best-of book. This will give you a better idea as to how the photographer tells a wedding story.

- Pay close attention to the style of photography and whether it matches what you have in mind for your own album.
- Does the album have a wide variety of shots?
- Look at the framing of each shot: Is the focal point in view, is it in focus?
- Consider the cohesiveness of an album as a whole: Do you get a good feel of the couple's wedding day?

☐ ask the photographer both basic and open-ended questions to get a sense of his personality:

- How many weddings do you shoot a year?
- What do you love most about shooting weddings?
- How long have you been in the business?
- What inspired you to become a wedding photographer?
- Do you use a digital or film camera? Why?

☐ don't forget to ask some specific business-minded questions:

- Will you be photographing the wedding solo, or will there be more than one photographer? If so, how will the responsibilities be divided?
- What is your backup plan in case of equipment failure? Illness?
- What are our options regarding packages?
- What's the turnaround time for proofs and final albums?
- How much do prints cost?
- How much do albums typically cost and what are our options?
- What's the process postwedding? (Do you provide online proofs or hard copies?)
- What sort of touch-ups do you do?
- What do you do with the high-resolution digital negatives?
- Do you offer mini albums? (They're small enough to fit in the palm of your hand, or in your purse.)
- Do you offer online proofing albums, so that my guests can buy prints without going through me?
- What is the payment policy?
- What is the cancellation policy?

☐ check references. ask previous clients the following questions:

- How satisfied were you with the final product?
- How would you rate their professionalism?
- Were there any surprises or problems? How were they taken care of?
- Did the photographer respond quickly to e-mails and phone calls?

☐ decide which photographer to go with and call to book them.

☐ have your photographer draft a contract for you. (See points page 129.)

Portraits

When you go to take formal photos, arrange it so that the largest group goes first, so that family can be dismissed as soon as possible. And give the list of must-have groupings to your photographer as early as possible.

- Couple with bride's extended family
- Couple with groom's extended family
- Couple with bride's immediate family
- Couple with groom's immediate family
- Couple with bride's parents
- Couple with groom's parents
- Couple with child attendants
- Couple with entire wedding party
- Bride with bridesmaids and groom with bridesmaids
- Groom with groomsmen and bride with groomsmen
- Bride with the maid of honor
- Groom with the best man
- Couple with wedding party
- Just the couple, and so on

Getting Ready

- Mom helping bride with one last detail, such as veil
- Detail of shoes, accessories, hair, garter, something borrowed, something blue
- Groom getting ready with Dad and pals (knotting the tie is a classic)

The Ceremony

- Bride and groom separately making their way to the ceremony
- An empty shot of the room
- Close-up of floral décor or details
- Ushers escorting parents to their seats
- Grandparents walking down the aisle
- Flower girl/ring bearer waiting to walk down the aisle
- Close-up of programs
- The bride just before her entrance
- The bride's and groom's hands as they exchange rings
- Exchanging vows
- A wide shot of the ceremony in progress from the back
- The ceremony kiss
- Bride and groom leaving ceremony site
- Bride and groom in limo backseat

The Reception

- Shot from outside the reception site
- Reception details (in color) such as the place cards, guest book, centerpieces, decorations, table settings, and favors
- Overhead shot of the venue
- Bride and groom's first dance
- Grandparents dancing
- Parents dancing
- Wedding party dancing
- Kids playing or dancing
- Bride laughing with bridesmaids
- Cake table
- Close-up of friends and family making toasts
- Bride and groom leaving, waving from the backseat of the getaway car

PHOTOGRAPHY CONTRACT POINTS

- Your names and contact information
- Wedding photographer's name and contact information
- Name of a substitute photographer in case of emergency
- Your wedding date, address of all locations you want him to shoot, and the photographer's expected arrival time at each site
- Number of hours your photographer is expected to work
- Number of cameras that will be used, and which formats
- Guaranteed backup camera in case of equipment failure
- Number of rolls or frames to be shot (color and black-and-white)
- Number of proofs you'll receive
- Length of time photographer will keep your negatives
- Schedule for delivering proofs and final packages
- Shot list (must-have shots)
- Style of photography (such as formal portraits, documentary, or a mix of both)
- Other details (e.g., number of albums you'll receive)
- Total cost
- Extra fees (including overtime)
- Reorder fees
- Deposit amount due
- Balance and date due
- Cancellation and refund policy
- All signatures

interviewing videographers

At your meeting, you'll want to assess the videographer on several levels—not only on the quality of their wedding videos, but also on their personal qualities. If you want to look relaxed on camera, it's important that your videographer makes you feel comfortable and relaxed in person.

☐ bring the following with you to the interview:

- Videographer's contact info
- Your budget
- Your ideas of what services you're looking for
- List of questions and a notepad

☐ view a sample video, and look for the following elements:

- Style of videography (Is it very cinematic, like a Hollywood movie, or does the video have a documentary feel?)
- Smooth editing and transitions between scenes
- Use of special effects
- Sound quality

☐ judge his demeanor and professionalism.

Do you want someone who is going to be outgoing and bold and interact with the crowd? Or someone subtler? This quality should be apparent in the interview. You can get a good idea of his personality with the following questions:

- How many weddings have you shot?
- What do you love most about wedding videography?
- What's your storytelling approach when it comes to taping a wedding?

VIDEOGRAPHY CONTRACT POINTS

Confirm all of the following information is included in your contract.

- Your names and contact information
- Videographer's company name and contact information
- Name of videographer and names of assistants
- Date of wedding
- Locations (rehearsal dinner, home, ceremony, reception) where the videographer will work, with exact addresses
- Starting times and exact number of hours he will work
- Number of cameras to be used
- In the event of equipment failure, a backup camera guarantee

- Number of videos you'll receive and complete package details
- Date your unedited video will be ready
- Date you'll receive your finished, edited video—plus approximate length
- Total cost (itemized)
- Overtime fee
- Reorder prices
- Special instructions (who the videographer must catch on tape, interview questions you'd like him to ask, special songs, specific effects that you do or don't want used)
- Deposit amount due
- Balance and date due
- Cancellation and refund policy
- All signatures

☐ also ask a few technical questions about their craft:

- What kind of camera will you use?
- How do you ensure good sound quality?
- Is there a separate sound and lighting person?
- Can you explain what effects you like to use and tell me about the benefits of using them? (You may not catch everything, but it helps to have a sense of what's what.)

☐ if you like the way the interview is going, plunge into the nitty-gritty details that you'll need to know about before you sign a contract:

- For how many hours will you shoot?
- What exactly does each video package include?
- How many cameras will you use?
- Does having more cameras cost more?
- Will you use tripods or handheld?
- How do you coordinate with a wedding photographer? Have you ever worked with [insert your photographer's name] before?
- Have you ever shot a wedding at my ceremony or reception site before? If so, can I see the tape?
- How will you know who's who when shooting?
- Will you shoot any other weddings during my wedding weekend? (Make sure there are no time constraints.)
- Will you be the person shooting my wedding? Or will it be one of your staff members? (Make sure to meet that person and see her work.)

NEW IDEAS

- Webcast your ceremony so that guests unable to attend can watch online.
- Ask for same-day edits where clips from the ceremony are screened at the reception.
- Hire your videographer to film your engagement photo session for a cool behind-the-scenes reel.
- Incorporate photos or clips from your childhood.

- How new is your equipment?
- How bright a light will you use? (If shooting requires the room lights to be on all evening, you'll lose the ambiance.)
- How do you deal with a low-light church or reception room?
- Will a backup camera be on hand?
- How many minutes is the final product?
- Do I get a DVD? How many?
- Can I have the raw footage?

☐ call references and ask the following:

- How satisfied were you with the final product?
- How would you rate their professionalism?
- Were there any surprises or problems? How were they taken care of?
- Did the videographer respond quickly to e-mails and phone calls?
- Would you recommend the videographer to a friend?

☐ choose a videographer and call to book.

☐ have your videographer draft and send you a contract.

☐ confirm contract details (see contract points sidebar on page 130).

countdown to your wedding day

Once you've booked the photographer and videographer, you'll have to keep track of a few details and take care of a few tasks leading up to the day of.

☐ talk to the photographer and videographer about what they'll wear (let them know the formality of the event, be it black-tie or casual).

☐ give them the date and an itinerary for the day.

☐ give them any pertinent reception details, such as a room diagram noting where significant friends and family can be found during the reception.

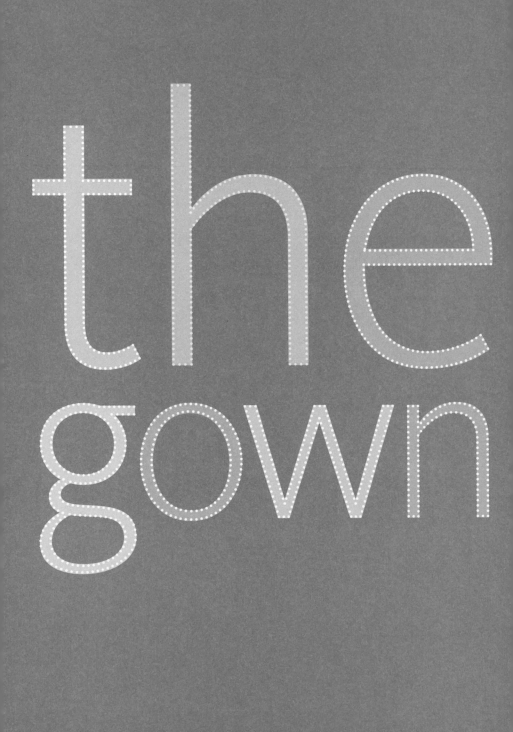

the
gown

{chapter 12}

What's the first thing people ask about when they hear you're getting married (after the obligatory, "What's the date?")? It never fails —it's always, "Have you bought your dress yet?" followed by, "What's it look like?" It's the most expensive, most stared-at piece of clothing you'll ever buy, so you have to find the dress that makes you feel giddy, beautiful, and sexy all at once. No pressure!

• Know your
approximate
wedding date

• Know your
reception and
ceremony site

browsing for gowns

There are so many gorgeous wedding dresses, it can make your head spin. So before you hit the bridal salons, look at gobs of pictures on TheKnot.com, where you can search by designer, color, and style. Then ask yourself some questions.

→ what's my wedding location?

You'll want to find a gown that's as formal as your locale. If you'll be on the beach, you'll want to opt out of a ball gown and find a sheath or slim A-line that's right for you.

→ what style gown am I looking for?

- **Princess** (You're as girly as it gets—think basque waists, ball gowns, tulle, and tons of embellishment.)
- **Traditional** (Your timeless look starts with your neckline, jewel or bateau, and a skirt with straight lines. Also on your checklist: your mother's pearls, a clutch, and proper pumps.)
- **Romantic** (*Pretty* is your operative word. You'll clothe yourself in a gown with intricate embroidery or layers of lace.)
- **Vintage** (You love the look of yesteryear: flutter cap sleeves, allover embellishment, and a slim but not form-fitting shape.)
- **Glamorous** (Get screen-star perfection with a body-skimming bias-cut dress, a low-cut back, and decadent jewel-studded accessories.)
- **Minimalist** (No bows, beads, or embroidery for you. You prefer to keep it simple with one show-off detail such as a unique fold to the fabric on your gown or an asymmetrical peak.)

→ what season am I marrying in?

Though most brides would wear a strapless gown any time of year, the climate will play a role in what fabric you choose. Generally speaking, silk satin or Mikado works well in all types of weather, while brocades and velvets work better in cold climates, and chiffons and linens in warmer ones.

Shortcut: TheKnot.com/gowns

→ what styles flatter my body type?

An experienced bridal salon consultant will be able to look at you and know what's going to look good, but it's smart to think about what styles (strapless, halter, drop waist) make you feel most comfortable. Here are some guidelines.

- **Busty:** Accentuate your features with a form-fitting scoop-neck bodice, and create balance with a full A-line skirt. Consider styles with natural or dropped waistlines to elongate your torso, while avoiding styles that maximize your chest, like Empire silhouettes.
- **Broad:** Go for a V-neck or sweetheart-style neckline. A slight dip in the center will draw the eye inward, elongating the neckline and de-emphasizing the bust. Steer clear of thin halters and off-the-shoulder styles that will exaggerate a wider frame.
- **Pear shaped:** Cover your bottom half with a ball gown or full A-line skirt and concentrate on highlighting your better half. A halter style will show off sexy shoulders, while a bateau neckline will make your top look more proportionate.
- **Full figured:** Try a ball gown with a basque waist, which has a slimming effect. A high-waisted A-line with a low neckline also flatters curves. Avoid dresses with lots of ruching or pickups; the extra fabric will add extra weight.
- **Boxy:** Empire waistlines are made with you in mind. Or, if you have your heart set on a ball gown, try creating an hourglass waistline with an interesting detail like an embellished ribbon or sash.
- **Petite:** Keep it simple with a columnlike sheath or an A-line, which both create uninterrupted lines. And stick to open necklines—think strapless and spaghetti-strap styles.
- **Tall:** You look great in anything from a sheath or A-line to a full ball gown. Accentuate your collarbone with a fitted bodice and open neckline.
- **Bony:** A small frame may get lost in all the fabric of a large ball gown. Go with a full A-line for the same dramatic look, and add some sex appeal with a low-dipped back. Self-conscious about an exposed collarbone? Try a structured sheath with a jewel (or T-shirt) neckline.

GOWN SILHOUETTES

Ball gown (The most traditional shape—think Cinderella before midnight.)

Sheath (A slim, body-hugging shape.)

A-line (It's cut narrow at the top and extends out along the body in a triangle shape.)

Fit-and-flare (A skirt that's slim in the hips but flares at the bottom.)

- **Pregnant:** Try to find a bridal salon that will be able to work with you and your timeline; or wait until the date gets closer and then find a dress off the rack, since you won't know your exact measurements when you order a custom-made gown. An Empire-waist dress is definitely your best bet, although some A-line silhouettes and ruched details will flatter your shape.

→ what length gown do I like?

- **Floor length:** Skirt falls to the floor.
- **Ballerina:** A full skirt that reaches to just above the ankles.
- **Tea length:** Hemmed to a few inches below the knee.
- **Hi-lo:** Has a shorter hem in the front and a floor-length hem in back.
- **Short, cocktail length:** Skirt hemmed above or at the knee.

→ what length train do I want?

- **Sweep:** Also called a "brush," it extends back 1½ feet or less from the gown.
- **Watteau:** It attaches to the gown at the shoulders and falls loosely to the hem.

- **Court:** Same length as a sweep train except that it extends from the waist.
- **Chapel:** Popular, it extends from 3½ to 4½ feet from the waist.
- **Cathedral:** A formal option, it extends 6½ to 7½ feet from the waist.
- **Monarch:** Also known as "royal," this version extends 12 or more feet from the waist.

→ what skirt details do I like?

- **Bustle:** Fabric gathered at the back, secured with buttons or hooks.
- **Draping:** Swaths of fabric pleated or gathered to a side or back seam of a skirt, adding fullness.
- **Flounce:** A wide ruffle around the bottom of a skirt.
- **Petal:** An overskirt of a different fabric that falls in rounded sections.
- **Pleats:** Folds of fabric pressed on top of each other like an accordion or a box shape.
- **Streamers:** Strings or ties that trail down the gown's back.
- **Tails:** Panels of the same or contrasting fabric, which trail behind the gown like a train.
- **Tiered:** A skirt made of fabric layers of various lengths.

WORDS TO KNOW

Fashion trends come and go, so here's the scoop on the latest silhouette styles:

- **Bias cut:** Cut on the diagonal, or bias, of the fabric.

- **Bubble:** It balloons out and then tapers in at the hem.

- **Fan back:** Has accordion pleats in the back, from just below the waist or knees.

- **Fishtail:** Has an additional, stitched-on panel in the back, like a fishtail.

- **Mermaid:** Slim and tapered, it follows the hip and flares out below the knees.

- **Trumpet:** Often confused with the mermaid, the big difference is that the straight-lined skirt subtly flares toward the hem in a trumpet shape at the knee.

- **Overskirt:** A second skirt partially covers the skirt beneath it.

→ which waistlines do I like?

- **Asymmetrical:** Features a change in waist height from one side to the other.
- **Basque:** Forms an elongated triangle below the natural waistline.
- **Dropped:** Falls several inches below the natural waistline.
- **Empire:** A high-waisted seam just below the bustline.
- **Natural:** The seam of the waistline lies, obviously, at the natural waist.

→ which necklines do I like?

- **Asymmetrical:** Neckline is different on either side of the center front; it could be a one-shoulder design.
- **Bateau:** Wide-necked shape follows the curve of the collarbone, almost to the tip of the shoulders.
- **Halter:** Straps wrap around the neck or has a high neck with deep armholes.
- **High collar:** Extends up the neck about one inch, better known as a mandarin collar.
- **Jewel:** Also known as the T-shirt neckline, it's round and sits at the base of the throat.
- **Off the shoulder:** Sits below the shoulders with sleeve-like straps that cover just the upper arm.
- **Portrait:** Has a wide, soft scoop from shoulder tip to shoulder tip.
- **Scoop:** A U-shaped style that can be cut low—the scoop often continues in the back.
- **Spaghetti strap:** Nearly strapless, save for the presence of thin, delicate straps.
- **Square:** Neckline is cut straight across the front.
- **Strapless:** Usually cut straight across, it can also peak on the sides or have a slight dip in the middle.
- **Sweetheart:** A low-cut neckline shaped like the top half of a heart, accenting the décolletage.
- **Tank:** Has a U-shaped neckline and deep armholes with narrow straps.
- **V-neck:** Dips down in the front in a flattering V shape.

→ do I want any embellishments?

Remember, less is more. Don't mix too many types of embellishment. Some to consider:

- **Appliqués:** Fabric elements stitched onto a gown; sometimes raised.
- **Beading:** Pieces of glass, crystal, gems, pearls, or other material sewn onto lace or fabric.
- **Border trim edging:** Braided, ribboned, ruffled, or scalloped edging.
- **Bows:** Used in various lengths and sizes.
- **Embroidery:** Fancy needlework patterns of fine threads stitched by hand or machine.
- **Fringe:** Ornamental trim consisting of loose strands of thread or beads, fastened to a band.
- **Laser cut:** Clean-edged intricate patterns cut into fabric via laser.
- **Quilting:** Sandwich of two layers of fabric over batting, which is then stitched in a pattern.
- **Sequins:** Tiny shiny, iridescent plastic disks sewn into place on a gown to add sparkle. Paillettes are larger versions of sequins, with a hole off-center at one end, sewn onto the gown to provide movement.

→ what colors look best with my skin tone?

Certain whites don't look right with some skin tones— you'd be amazed at the difference between diamond white and ecru.

- **Fair skin:** You'll look best in yellow ivories and warmer natural colors. Steer clear of stark diamond white, as it may wash you out.
- **Medium skin/pink undertones:** Opt for creamier colors.
- **Medium skin/yellow undertones:** Natural whites or champagne will look best.
- **Dark skin/yellow or olive undertones:** Go for stark white or champagne hues and stay away from yellow ivory.
- **Dark skin:** Most shades of white will complement your skin color.

→ what style veil do I like?

- **Blusher:** A short, single layer that's worn over the face before the ceremony, then either flipped over the head or removed.
- **Chapel:** A formal style that extends to the floor, it falls 2½ yards from the headpiece.
- **Cathedral:** One of the most formal veils available, it falls 3½ yards from the headpiece.
- **Elbow:** Extends to the bride's elbow.
- **Fingertip:** Good for ball gowns, it extends to the fingertips.
- **Flyaway:** Multilayered veil that just brushes the shoulders, considered less formal.
- **Mantilla:** Long, circular piece of lace that frames the face, usually secured with a comb.
- **Waltz:** A veil that falls somewhere between the knee and ankle.

→ do I have any religious restrictions?

Check with your ceremony officiant to find out whether there are any attire guidelines, such as covering your shoulders, at your house of worship.

shopping for a gown

Now that you're armed with this amazing (possibly overwhelming) list of choices, head to a bridal salon to try on gowns. Our best advice: Though it's essential to have a vision of your dream dress in your head, be open-minded. You never know which style is going to become *the one*. Much of your dress will be based on what designers the bridal salons carry. Here's how to get started:

☐ choose three salons to visit.

There are small boutiques, department stores, and many in between. Get a feel for what's out there:

- Search online and in the local listings area at TheKnot.com/bridalsalons.

- Ask friends where they shopped.
- Found designers you love? Find out which stores carry them.

☐ call salons to make appointments.

If possible, make appointments for evenings or weekdays when the salon won't be so crowded—you'll get more one-on-one time. But first confirm the following:

- Whether you need an appointment (most often you will)
- Price range of the lines they carry
- Length of time to order a gown
- Whether you'll be assigned a sales associate
- Whether you'll be able to peruse the racks, or the sales associate will do it for you
- If there's a limit on the number of gowns you can try on
- What you need to bring (undergarments, shoes, etc.)
- What size sample dresses are available
- What designers they carry

☐ come to your appointment prepared.

Bring:

- Photos of dresses you've seen online or in magazines that you absolutely love
- Your mom, your maid of honor, and/or a brutally honest friend (no more than three people, though)
- A strapless bra or bustier
- Control-top panty hose (so gowns go on more smoothly, especially the often-too-small sample sizes)
- A slip if you plan to try on sheaths or slip dresses
- Shoes with approximately the same heel height you plan to wear on your wedding day
- A hair tie to put your hair up

5 ALTERNATIVES TO A VEIL

1. One or two skinny headbands
2. Fresh flowers
3. Vintage hair comb
4. Barrettes made out of shell, like mother of pearl
5. Hair sticks with sparkle

☐ try on gowns.

We know it sounds a little obvious, but there are some important tips to consider when gown shopping.

- Don't eliminate anything at first glance. It helps to try on all different kinds of dresses, and then to decide which shape and style you look and feel best in. So if the salesperson brings you something she says you must try—try it.
- If you have to be reassured that the gown looks great on you, it's probably not the one. Can you really see yourself walking down the aisle swathed in this gown? If not, take it off and move on.
- Even after you think you've found your gown, take a day to be absolutely sure it's the one for you. Since bridal gowns are custom-made, most salons put a no-return policy in their contracts.

☐ once you find a gown you like, ask the following:

- Can I see a fabric sample of the gown I want to order? (Store samples can be worn from wear, and the color may not be true.)
- What are the appropriate accessories (matching veil, headpiece)?
- Do you sell accessories to complement the gown or can you suggest someone who does?
- Can I get a written estimate of alterations when I order the dress?
- What are the appropriate undergarments for this dress (bustier, bra, slimmer)?

☐ make sure to request a letter of agreement with the receipt and that it includes the following points:

- Your name and contact info
- Salesperson name and contact info
- Your wedding date
- A detailed description of your gown
- Size or measurements the salon is sending to the manufacturer

- Written alterations list and estimate
- Approximate delivery date
- Itemized price for gown
- Number of fittings included in the price (if any)
- Amount of deposit and date paid
- Amount of money owed on the gown and date due
- Cancellation and refund policy
- Any other services requested such as steaming or gown preservation

☐ pay with a credit card. if something goes wrong with the gown, you'll want to be able to dispute a payment.

☐ when you purchase the gown, ask:

- If there's a bustle, can you demonstrate how it works, so the maid of honor can learn?
- How do I banish last-minute wrinkles: Should I use an iron? On what setting? Is steaming a better option?
- What if I spill something on the gown? Are there certain products I should or shouldn't use?

alterations and accessories

Buying your gown is the first step; then you have to make it fit. The alterations process is more than just hemming and cinching—you need to have all your fashion elements at the ready to make sure they work with your overall look (remember, you won't have seen the dress for many months).

☐ buy proper undergarments.

They can't fit the gown without them. It's worth it to splurge on high-quality items so there are no visible bumps or seams. Consider the following:

- bra
- bustier
- stockings
- thong
- slimmer

☐ buy your shoes.

Accurate height is essential when having your gown hemmed. (It's also a good idea to break them in before the wedding day.)

☐ buy your accessories.

It's best to limit yourself to one show-stopping piece.

- Necklace
- Earrings
- Bracelet
- Ring
- Hairpins
- Hair accessories

☐ have your first fitting (6 weeks before the wedding).

Ensure that the gown is the right size, color, and design. Try on all your accessories with the gown to make sure you like the overall look. Things to consider during this fitting:

- Do I like the way the material falls?
- How do I like the way it fits in the bust, waist, and so on?
- Is there any puckering, bunching, or bulging?
- Does everything seem well sewn?
- Speak up if you see something you don't like. This is your time to be demanding.
- Schedule your second fitting before you leave the salon.

☐ have your second fitting (one month before the wedding).

Bring your foundation garments, shoes, jewelry, and any other accessories you plan to wear. And make sure all your concerns from the first fitting have been addressed and fixed:

- Can I move comfortably? (Walk around the salon to make sure.)
- Does everything stay in place?
- Any obvious bunching or wrinkling?
- Once again, speak up if there's something you don't like.

If there is a problem, continue to schedule fittings until you are completely satisfied.

☐ have the final fitting (one to two weeks before the wedding day).

- Go through a run-through to make sure your maid of honor knows how to bustle your dress.
- Get rid of any last-minute wrinkles at this time. Ask if it's okay to iron any part of the gown.
- When your appointment is over, schedule a date and time within one week of your wedding to pick up your gown.

☐ dress on your wedding day.

Figure out where you'll get dressed the day of. Also, determine who will deliver the gown to this location. Be prepared for any last-minute issues like steaming.

WAYS TO SAVE

Gowns can range from $500 to $5,000 and much much more. But before you throw in the tulle, try one of these alternate routes:

- **Simplify your style:** If your dream gown is superembellished, ask if the designer has a similar style without the extra beading (which increases the price).

- **Go to sample sales:** Get on the mailing list for your favorite salons or designer shops. Ask if and when they have sample sales. You can get up to a 75 percent discount.

- **Ask other brides:** You'd be surprised how many brides hate their gown once it arrives. Many choose to get a new one at the last minute. Peruse TheKnot.com's message boards or eBay sites for gowns that have never been worn.

- **Check out consignment shops:** High-end thrift stores may carry a once-worn designer gown.

styling your hair and makeup

Up or down? Tight or loose? Short or long? As endless as they may seem, these are all questions you must ask when deciding on a wedding day hairstyle. To help make the decision a little more manageable, consider these questions:

why something old, new, borrowed, and blue?

Something old represents a bride's bond to her family and old life; something new shows her new good fortune; something borrowed from another bride is supposed to bring good luck; and something blue dates back to biblical times when the color blue meant purity and fidelity.

→ what do I want to look like on my wedding day?

Browse wedding magazines and websites for hair and makeup styles that best complement you and your wedding.

→ where and what time of day is my wedding?

Your wedding locale and time are major factors to consider. Loose locks and a bronzed, dewy look are perfect for a beach wedding, but not right for a grand ballroom affair.

→ what is the overall style of my wedding?

Your hair and makeup are just as much a part of the day as your centerpieces and your cake, so you want them to tie in with the overarching theme of your wedding. Laid-back romantic wedding? Leave your hair loose or down. And do the opposite for a formal affair.

→ what are my day-to-day beauty considerations?

Think about the issues you encounter during your daily routine and choose a look accordingly. (Does jet-black mascara give you unsightly under-eye circles?) Sure you can touch up smudges and curls throughout the day, but will you really want to?

→ do I want to wear any hair accessories?

Whether it's a tiara or a veil or a simple flower tucked behind the ear, it's easier if you know how you'll be accessorizing your hair *before* falling in love with a style.

finding a hairstylist and makeup artist

You don't have to be a total diva to know that good help is hard to find. Talented hair and makeup stylists are no exception, so here's how to start:

☐ do your research.

- Talk to friends who always look great. Nothing beats word-of-mouth when it comes to finding a skilled beauty team.

- Hit up the beauty consultants at cosmetics counters and pay attention to their look. If you feel comfortable with them, ask for a free makeover.
- Browse online for local hairstylists and makeup artists. Also, make a list of beauty salons to call, and don't forget to ask if they have people who do makeup on staff.
- Talk to your photographer. Most photographers have worked with reputable hair and makeup people and will often recommend them if asked.
- If you live in a major city like New York or Los Angeles, call up a few agents who represent hairstylists and makeup artists, and see if they can make any suggestions.
- Already have a hairstylist? Ask if she knows anyone who does makeup and vice versa. You'd be amazed how much they cross over.

☐ set up consultation appointments.

Call the beauty salons you have in mind, and let them know you want to schedule a consultation for your wedding day hair and/or makeup. Be sure to bring pictures of styles and looks that you like so the stylist has an idea of what you're going for. Ask yourself:

- Do they understand what I want?
- Can I trust them to achieve the results I'm after? (A trial run will help assuage any concerns.)
- Do they have good suggestions for my hair and skin type?

☐ find out the details.

- Can you come to my home/getting-ready spot?
- Will you charge a higher fee to come to my home than if I go to the salon? Am I expected to pay travel expenses?
- What will happen if you can't be there on the day of my wedding? Will you arrange for someone else to do the job, or am I on my own?
- Can you do the bridal party's hair as well, or just mine?
- Can you stay with me throughout the day to do touch-ups before the ceremony and photo session?
- Can we do a trial run? Is there a fee?
- Do you charge per person or a daily rate?

☐ book your hairstylist and makeup artist.

Once you've had consultations with all your potential hair and makeup artists, decide which one you like best and call to book them for your wedding day. Make sure your hair and makeup contract(s) include these important points:

- Date any to-be-determined details will be confirmed to stylist in writing
- Wedding date, including day of week
- Time the stylists should arrive, or your appointment time if you're going to them
- Detailed description of what stylist will be doing
- Price and payment schedule
- Outline of what the price includes
- Refund policy

☐ have a trial run.

If you're not completely certain about your beauty team, you may want to schedule a trial appointment before you book, and you will probably have to pay for this. During this session, the stylists will create versions of your actual wedding-day look, so if there's something specific you're looking for, you'll want to speak up.

- **Wear white:** Wear a top with a color and neckline that's similar to your gown, so you can see the total look.
- **Bring your wedding day musts:** Bring your veil, earrings, and headpiece to figure out how they'll fit with your 'do.
- **Take examples:** Bring pictures of what you do and don't like to better explain your vision.
- **Snap photos:** Don't forget your digital camera to ensure you like the style from every angle.
- **Time it right:** Try to schedule your trials before your prewedding parties or other special events. Most stylists charge for these practice runs, so find a crowd to wow.
- **Check back:** Take a close look at yourself a few hours after a trial makeover to check how the hairstyle and makeup last.
- **Watch the clock:** Be aware of how long your style takes so you can set up your wedding day itinerary. Allow the

timed amount plus a half an hour in your day-of schedule, so you won't be rushed.

☐ check in with your wedding party.

Find out who in your wedding party wants to get their hair and makeup done (typically, they cover the cost). When it comes to hair, the stylist will need to know ahead of time who's getting an updo and who's keeping it down for pricing and scheduling.

☐ create a beauty timeline.

Once you know everyone's needs, set up a day-of schedule. Allow for extra time in case of hair or makeup emergencies (especially redos). Depending on the number of stylists, some girls may have to get ready superearly, so let them know ahead of time. You, the bride, should be saved for last.

☐ prepare a wedding-day beauty kit.

For makeup, don't waver from products you normally use. And leave products you've never used before at home— your wedding day is not the time to discover new allergies. Be prepared for any emergencies by arming one of your bridesmaids with these items packed in a midsize beauty bag (see page 191 for an extensive emergency kit list):

- A few tissues, cotton balls, and cotton swabs
- Bobby pins
- Breath mints/spray
- Concealer/cover-up
- Dental floss
- Deodorant
- Eye drops
- Hairbrush
- Hair spray

- Hand cream
- Lip gloss or lip balm
- Lip liner
- Lipstick
- Mascara
- Nail polish
- Your perfume
- Toothbrush and toothpaste

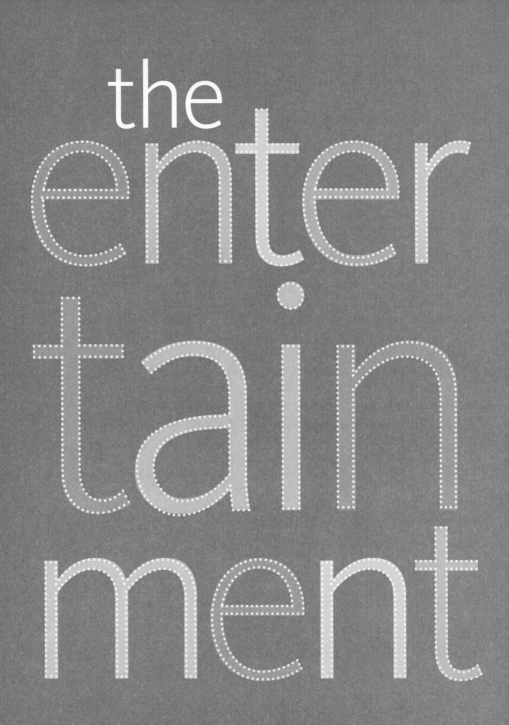

the
enter
tain
ment

{ chapter 13 }

Sure your dress should be to die for and your wedding color-palette perfect, but at the end of the party, it's the music that makes your wedding memorable. The big question: Will you hire a swinging big band, or a hip scratching DJ? Think about your preference, then book your tunes right away.

determining your music style

It's true, the music—literally—sets the tone of the reception. Hip-hop, swing, jazz, and oldies all create a different vibe. While you can mix genres, you need to focus on what type of musicians you want to dance to all night long. Answer these questions:

→ **do we want a DJ or a band?**

There are advantages to both. With a band, you'll have that live music energy and sound, while a DJ has access to a wide range of songs and genres performed exactly as you remember them. Want the best of both worlds? Hire a band for the start of the night and a DJ for the after party.

→ **if we have a band, what kind of sound do we want?**

Look to your musical tastes, locale, and guests when answering this question. Showcasing a specific sound will help set your overall wedding ambiance. A few to consider:

- Big band
- Jazz band
- Motown band
- Country band
- Cover band
- Latin band
- Oldies band
- Reggae band
- Rock band
- Swing band
- Top 40 band
- Traditional wedding band (a wide range of genres)

→ **if we choose a DJ, what type of DJ do we want?**

- Turntable DJ (uses actual records or CDs)
- Radio DJ (uses a number of sound sources, including CDs and digital music files)

→ if there will be a cocktail hour, what music do we want played during this time?

You can go a couple of ways with this:

- Use the musicians from your ceremony (especially if cocktails will be served near the ceremony site).
- Let your reception band or DJ take care of the cocktail hour. (You could enlist a few members of the band to arrive early to play during this time, for example.)
- Hire a completely different group to play for just one hour. (This could be a group that reflects your culture, like a salsa band, or one that enhances the locale, like a reggae group for a Jamaican wedding.)

→ how much entertainment/interaction do we want our musicians or DJ to provide?

Decide whether you want your band or DJ to make announcements, or to just provide music. If you want someone who can really work the crowd, you'll be looking for a very different personality than if you want someone whose interaction with the crowd is minimal.

7 WAYS TO PERSONALIZE YOUR RECEPTION MUSIC

1. Use your parents' first dance song as yours.
2. Have anniversary dances for all your relatives.
3. Have the DJ or bandleader explain the significance behind your first dance song.
4. Choreograph your first dance song.
5. If you play an instrument or sing, do a surprise performance.
6. Play a three-song homage to your state (Bon Jovi's hits = New Jersey; John Denver = Colorado).
7. Choose entrance songs for each of your attendants.

finding reception bands/DJs

Once you've nailed down your reception music criteria, you'll want to get started seeking out bands or DJs. As always, get recommendations from recently married friends and local listings on TheKnot.com/music. Also, look for entertainment companies that represent many bands and DJs in your area and can help you pinpoint the sounds you're looking for. Here's a rundown of the steps to take:

☐ determine your entertainment budget.

About 10 percent of your overall budget should be allotted for your entertainment.

☐ listen to music samples.

Look online for demos to download and listen to so that you can get a sense of their overall style. Notice what type of music they play most—this is probably what they're most used to playing, so make sure you like it.

☐ see them perform.

If possible, go check out bands and DJs live at a showcase— it's the best way to determine whether they're right for your reception.

☐ call bands, booking agents, or DJs to make appointments.

But first confirm the following:

- Wedding date availability
- The number of acts they represent (if it's a booking agent)
- Price range
- Playlist capabilities

☐ meet with prospective musicians or their agent.

At your meeting, you'll want to assess the band or DJ on several levels—not only judging their level of playing or their playlists, but also their personalities. Is this a group of people or person that will be entertaining or annoying? Kick things off with some general questions:

- What type of events do you most often play/host?
- How long have you played music?
- What was the most unique performance/reception you ever played?
- For an agent: How many bands and DJs do you represent?

☐ listen to demos or watch wedding performances.

Ask about their music preferences:

- Do you have set songs to choose from?
- Can we completely customize our playlist?
- Will you learn new songs?
- Do you take requests from guests?
- Do you know any of the traditional/cultural songs we want played?
- What types of songs do you think would be appropriate for our wedding style and the age range of our guests?
- Will the musicians we're hearing on this demo be the same ones at our wedding?

☐ ask about equipment and setup.

- Have you performed at our site before?
- What sort of equipment or setup do you require?
- Do you use special lighting?
- Can you provide a wireless microphone for the toasts?
- How do you charge? By the hour? By the event?
- What are your overtime fees?
- How soon before the reception will you arrive?

☐ ask about the number of musicians in the band.

Some bands will let you add or reduce the number of players from the core band. It's obviously less expensive to have fewer musicians, but ask how the sound quality will be affected. If you love the band for the bluesy trombone sound, will he stay?

☐ find out about their reception backup plan.

- If you're ill on the day of the wedding, who will be your substitute? Can I meet him?

☐ Confirm reception details:

- Will you need time to warm up?
- Who will be the emcee?
- How do you take breaks (Do you play recorded music in between sets? Or do you rotate members for constant live music?)
- What will you wear?
- Do you require special meals?

☐ ask for references.

When it comes to your band, it's a great idea to get first-hand information from another couple. If you didn't hear about the band/DJ from a person you trust, call the references and ask:

- Were you happy with the overall performance?
- Were there any problems?
- Did they accommodate your requests?
- What sort of feedback did you get from your guests about the music?

☐ book the band.

Have the band/DJ draft a contract outlining everything you talked about and send it to you. Confirm all of the following is included in your band/DJ contract:

- Your names and contact information
- Your wedding date, time, phone number
- Your reception location address
- Band/DJ company name and contact information
- Actual names of DJ or band members, including the names of all the key members
- Detailed description of your reception music
- Must-play songs
- No-play songs
- Emcee instructions

- What they will supply in terms of equipment (microphones, sound system)
- Breaks to be taken (how long, whether music will be played during that time)
- Any other agreements you may have made orally
- Cancellation and refund policy
- Total cost and an itemized breakdown of what's included
- Deposit amount
- Payments to be made, in what form, and dates due
- To whom checks should be made out
- All signatures

☐ review the contract, sign it, and return it with your deposit.

☐ pay the full amount two weeks beforehand, or by whatever date has been decided on.

creating your playlist and reception plan

About two months before the wedding, you'll need to sit down and create your must-have songs, especially if your band has agreed to learn a new tune.

☐ write down your must-play songs.

Look at the band's or DJ's list and pick ten to fifteen gotta-have-it songs. You need to give your musicians some freedom to read the crowd and know what will be a hit.

☐ clue them in to your first dance song and any other special songs.

This will fall into your timeline, but if you have a specific request for how your first dance song should be played (e.g., eliminate the verse about breaking up) you'll need to give them plenty of warning.

☐ are there any do-not-play songs?

If the "Chicken Dance" gives you hives, by all means, put it on your no-play list. Don't overwhelm them with a tirade on why pop music is the pits. Pick a few songs that really drive you crazy, and in a meeting explain what genres of music you do and do not like.

☐ do we have any cultural music traditions we want to have our band or DJ play?

Will you have a dollar dance, or a *hora*? Plan arrangements with your DJ or bandleader to make sure these traditions aren't overlooked at the reception.

☐ decide where they'll set up.

Talk to your reception site manager to figure out the best place for the band/DJ to set up. Keep in mind that they'll be bringing some hefty equipment and will need access to a large door into the room.

☐ coordinate arrival times to the reception site.

If you're hiring a DJ or a band that needs time to set up,

YOUR RECEPTION EMCEE

Consider that fact that whomever you hire to provide the music will probably be the same person who emcees the reception. It's a good idea to give your DJ or band-leader a list of events and what needs to be said at what time. Here's an outline of what you might want announced:

- Bride and groom entrance, requested music (with exactly how you would like to be introduced)
- Other entrances, requested songs: Bridal party entrance, Parents of the bride, Parents of the groom, Grand-parents, etc.

- Blessing and who is giving it
- First toast and who is giving it
- First dance and requested song
- People to join in on first dance and requested song
- Father-daughter dance and requested song
- Mother-son dance and requested song
- Open dance floor for guests
- Cake cutting and requested song
- Last dance and requested song

make sure that the reception site knows and okays their arrival time. And let your band or DJ know the exact room name at your reception site.

☐ make timeline decisions.

Decide when you want to be announced and when you want to cut the cake. Then use your emcee list of announcements (prevoius page) to fill in the times. Get that information to your reception site manager and your DJ or bandleader.

TOP 10 CLASSIC FIRST DANCE SONGS

1. "At Last," Etta James
2. "Unforgettable," Nat King Cole
3. "The Way You Look Tonight," Frank Sinatra
4. "It Had to Be You," Harry Connick, Jr.
5. "From This Moment," Shania Twain
6. "What a Wonderful World," Louis Armstrong
7. "Endless Love," Diana Ross and Lionel Richie
8. "Can't Help Falling in Love," Elvis Presley
9. "I Will," The Beatles
10. "As Time Goes By," from *Casablanca*

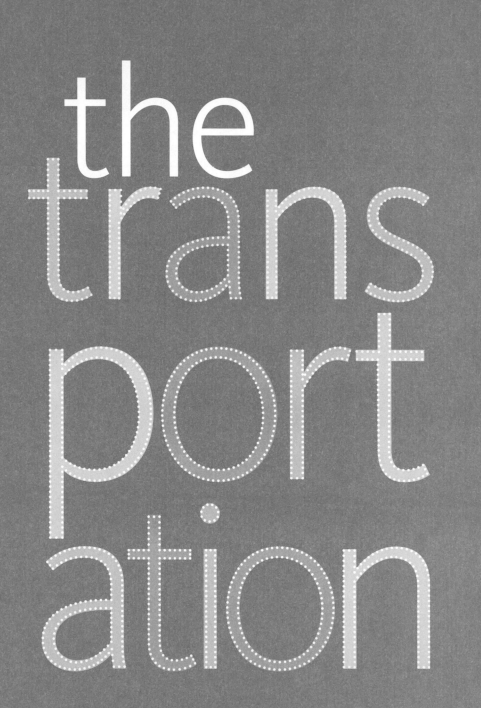

the
trans
port
ation

{ chapter 14 }

Like the song says, you're going to the chapel
to do you-know-what. But how are you
getting there? How is your mom, for that
matter? Whatever wedding wheels you
choose, make sure that they fit with your style
and theme. Will you choose a sleek, silver
Rolls-Royce, a horse and buggy, or will you
just walk yourselves down the road? We have
tips on how to get rolling on all your
transportation needs.

• Know your
wedding date

• Know your
ceremony and
reception
location

finding your transportation style

Before you go booking any old limousine, ask yourselves these questions:

→ **who do we need to accommodate? and how many people will that be?**

- Just the two of us
- The wedding party
- Parents, grandparents, and immediate family
- All the guests

→ **what do we need transportation for?**

- To the ceremony
- To the reception from the ceremony
- From the reception to the hotel/after party
- From the after party to the hotel
- To and from any other prewedding events (welcome party or rehearsal dinner)

→ **what's our wedding style?**

Take your style into account when deciding on your ride.

- Romantic fairy tale (leave by carriage or in a vintage car)
- Formal, black-tie (drive away in a Rolls-Royce or other luxury car)
- Laid-back natural (walk or ride bikes, or hop on a trolley)
- Simple traditional (book a limo with all the amenities)

→ **do we know anyone we can borrow from?**

Does your dad's friend love showing off his cherry red Lamborghini or a silver BMW Z3 roadster? Or does your best friend's dad just happen to have a boat fit for your waterside reception? Ask if he can be your chauffeur (or let you borrow it).

Shortcut: TheKnot.com/transportation

booking your transportation

Once you have a better idea of what you're looking for, collect the names of transportation companies from friends, recent newlyweds, other vendors, and TheKnot.com/transportation. Or, call the National Limousine Association for referrals. Once you've found companies that can carry your crowd (and are available on your day), narrow down your choices.

NEW IDEAS

* Zip away on a motorcycle or a chic Vespa
* Go all out with a helicopter escape
* Sail away in a canoe for two
* Motor off on an old-fashioned tractor

☐ ask about pricing.

- Is there a minimum time/price requirement?
- Is gratuity included?
- How much will you save if the driver drops you off and returns later, as opposed to staying the whole time?
- Does the clock start at pickup, or from the driver's original destination?
- Are specialty cars available? How much more do they cost?
- What are the overtime charges?
- Are there any wedding discounts? (What if you book the same company for your bachelor and bachelorette parties as well?)
- What comes with the rental? (Will there be a TV in the limo? Champagne? Snacks?)
- What are the cancellation/refund policies?

☐ check out their fleet.

- How many passengers can the vehicles comfortably fit?
- How old are the cars?
- Can you secure a color preference?

☐ assess their reliability

- Will they be handling other big events on that day?
- Is the driver familiar with the area?
- Will the driver have a map or GPS in the car? Does the car have a spare tire, jack, etc. in case of an emergency?
- Do I need to provide directions?
- Will the driver call when he is on the way or when he arrives?

- What if the driver is late? Will you send a backup car?
- How will the driver be dressed?

finalizing your transportation plan

Once you've found a car company you trust, provide them with all the information they'll need for a smooth ride.

☐ **designate a transportation point person.**

If you don't have a wedding planner, ask someone in your wedding party. She should be in charge of making sure everyone gets picked up and dropped off according to schedule and have the driver's cell phone number just in case.

☐ **test-drive your routes.**

A practice run will give you a better idea of when to schedule pickup times. Try to do it the same time of day as your wedding to get a good sense of traffic or construction obstacles.

☐ **create a transportation timeline.**

Include those who need transporting, contact numbers, times, and exact locations. Fax this to the car company ahead of time, and, on the wedding day, give a copy to the driver and your wedding party point person.

☐ **decide on any amenities/décor.**

Let the car company know if you have a special request (you'll be bringing sparklers back into the car after the ceremony, for instance).

☐ **confirm arrangements the day before the wedding.**

Get an after-hours phone number of someone at the limo company in case of any emergencies.

☐ reserve parking.

Some guests will be shuttling themselves around, so don't forget about parking. Talk to the reception site manager and find out what your parking options are, and who handles the arrangements and staff.

☐ make sure everything is on schedule.

Have your point person call twenty to thirty minutes ahead of pickup time to make sure the driver will be arriving on time.

TRANSPORTATION COMPANY CONTRACT POINTS

* Your names and contact information
* Transportation company contact information
* Your wedding date, time, and phone number of site
* Your wedding-day driver and his work attire
* An itemized list of the cars being rented (with makes, models, and colors), hours requested for pickup and departure, and rates (including minimum rentals)

* Confirmation of dates, times, and locations for pickups and drop-offs
* A contact phone number for someone in the bridal party
* Amenities to be in the car upon arrival
* Deposit amount and due date
* Balance amount and due date
* Total cost (including tax)
* Amount of overtime charges per hour
* Cancellation and refund policies
* All signatures

{ chapter 15 }

Contrary to popular belief, wedding gifts aren't mandatory—though very much appreciated. While some brides and grooms feel awkward about registering for specific items, in reality it's a big relief for guests who haven't a clue what you may like or what you already have! Think of this as your opportunity to clean out the closets and start fresh with items you'll *both* love.

BEFORE
YOU BEGIN

• Know your
  wedding date
• Know your
  pre- and post-
  wedding home
  addresses

creating your registry plan

Friends and relatives will be looking to buy gifts for all those prewedding and engagement bashes, so you want to make sure to register your wishes prior to your shower or even engagement party. You don't need to complete your list just yet, but at least have a selection for guests to browse by the six-month mark.

☐ do it together.

Talk about the style of home you'd both like, and split up the final say (you could alternate items) to make it fair. Maybe he gets to make final decisions on electronics, while you get to choose the kitchen stuff since you're the chef.

☐ take inventory.

Before you go scanner-gun happy at every department store in town, do a little homework on the items that you'll need most. See our list on page 172–173.

☐ choose more than one store.

One is not enough, ten is too many. Two to four registries give guests more choices, and it's a manageable number. To make it easy on yourself and others, pick one store for bedding, another for china, and so on. This will prevent you from signing up for the same items at different stores.

☐ interview the store.

Get a feel for how its registry operates and what the customer service is like. Ask:

• What range of products and brands does the registry carry? Is every item in the store available for the registry?
• Will you ship to the address we designate? Can you send gifts in a batch?
• Can our guests buy online?
• How will the retailer keep track of our registry?

- How long after a gift is bought will the purchase be reflected on the list? (Big retailers should have a computerized system that is updated instantly.)
- How long is the exchange/return period? What are the terms? (This is crucial. You don't want to end up with any duplicates or get back from your honeymoon and find out you have only ten days left to exchange or return any items you don't want.)
- Are there any perks for registering there? (Some offer a completion program that allows you to purchase whatever you don't receive at a discount.)
- How long will our registry stay active?

finalizing your registry lists

It's time to start scanning: Make a plan to register at a few stores to create a selection of gifts that suits your needs. Once you've registered, the key is getting the word out so guests know where to buy gifts.

☐ set up a time to register.

Many stores offer special hours for couples to register. Take advantage of it; and don't try to register all at once. You can always start a registry in the store and finish it up online.

☐ know your guests.

Register for gifts at a variety of price points: under $50, under $75, under $100, under $200, and beyond.

☐ over-register.

It's better to over-register than not to register for enough. If you get things you don't love, return them for store credit and get something you love later. Plan on registering for two to three gifts per guest on your list.

{ registry checklist }

Ask yourselves some questions to avoid the slightest registry remorse.

→ what kitchenware do we need?

- ☐ Blender
- ☐ Coffeemaker
- ☐ Coffee grinder
- ☐ Teakettle
- ☐ Food processor
- ☐ Hand mixer
- ☐ Slow cooker
- ☐ Toaster
- ☐ 4- or 5-inch skillet
- ☐ 10- or 12-inch skillet
- ☐ 2- or 3-quart saucepan with lid
- ☐ Stockpot with pasta insert
- ☐ Dutch oven (4 or 6 quart)
- ☐ Roasting pan
- ☐ Steamer insert
- ☐ Colander
- ☐ Casserole dish

→ what baking items do we want?

- ☐ Baking sheets, cake pans, and muffin tins (2 each)
- ☐ Nesting bowls
- ☐ Measuring cups/spoons

→ what knives do we need?

- ☐ Set of steak knives
- ☐ Chef's knife (between 6 and 12 inches)
- ☐ Paring knife (between 2½ and 4 inches)
- ☐ Utility knife (between 4 and 7 inches)
- ☐ Sharpening tool
- ☐ Pair of kitchen shears

→ what tableware do we need?

- ☐ Casual place settings for 12: dinner plate, salad/dessert plate, soup/cereal bowl, mug
- ☐ Salt and pepper shakers
- ☐ Serving platter
- ☐ Sugar bowl and creamer
- ☐ Serving bowls (2 or 3)
- ☐ Salad bowl
- ☐ Serving trays (2)
- ☐ Soup tureen
- ☐ Butter dish
- ☐ Cake plate
- ☐ Espresso cups and saucers (8)
- ☐ Accent plates (12)

→ how much silverware do we need?

- ☐ 5-piece flatware settings for 13: Formal and casual sets should each have a dinner fork, salad fork, tablespoon, teaspoon, and knife
- ☐ Butter knife
- ☐ Salad servers
- ☐ Serving spoons (2)
- ☐ Slotted serving spoon
- ☐ Serving forks (2)
- ☐ Ladle
- ☐ Demitasse spoons (8)

→ are we registering for fine china? if so, what do we want?

- ☐ Formal china place settings for 12: dinner plate, salad/dessert plate, bread and butter plate, teacup, and saucer
- ☐ Rimmed soup bowls that double as pasta bowls (12)

- [ ] Chargers (12)
- [ ] Coffeepot
- [ ] Teapot
- [ ] Gravy boat and stand

→ **what glassware and barware do we want?**

- [ ] Wineglasses (14) 2 extra for breakage
- [ ] Water goblets (14)
- [ ] Champagne flutes (12)
- [ ] Double old-fashioned glasses (12)
- [ ] Iced beverage glasses (12)
- [ ] Margarita glasses (6)
- [ ] Martini glasses (6)
- [ ] Dessert wineglasses (6)
- [ ] Shot glasses (6)
- [ ] Highballs (12)
- [ ] Juice glasses (6)
- [ ] Beer mugs or pilsners (6)
- [ ] Casual drinking glasses (12)
- [ ] Cocktail shaker
- [ ] Ice bucket and tongs
- [ ] Jigger and bar tools

→ **what bedroom items do we need?**

- [ ] Sheet sets (4)
- [ ] Duvet or down comforter
- [ ] Bedcover
- [ ] Bed skirt
- [ ] Mattress pads (2)
- [ ] Blankets (2)
- [ ] Pillows (6)
- [ ] Decorative pillows (2 or 3)

→ **what do we need for the dining room?**

- [ ] Napkins (12)
- [ ] Large formal tablecloth
- [ ] Casual napkins and placemats (12)
- [ ] Cotton or pad liner for tablecloth
- [ ] Smaller tablecloths and napkins

→ **what do we need for the bathroom?**

- [ ] Bath towels (6)
- [ ] Bath sheets (6)
- [ ] Hand towels (6)
- [ ] Washcloths (4)
- [ ] Guest towels (4)
- [ ] Bath mat
- [ ] Shower curtain
- [ ] Scale
- [ ] Hamper

→ **what unconventional items could we use?**

- [ ] Barbecue grill
- [ ] Luggage
- [ ] Speakers for your iPod
- [ ] Digital camera
- [ ] Wall art
- [ ] Games (board games and outdoor games)
- [ ] Iron
- [ ] Ice-cream maker
- [ ] Bookcases

tradition trivia
Guests used to
bring fruits as their
gifts to the newly-
weds to encourage
fertility.

☐ check the list.

Once you've created your registry list, ask for a master list and read it carefully to make sure there are no mistakes. Get the business card of the person who helped you set up the program, so that you have a point person should you have any questions or problems.

☐ confirm the facts.

Double-check recipient names and the mailing address for where gifts will be sent.

☐ spread the word.

Inform parents, attendants, and key friends where you're registered. Include where you're registered on your website and shower invitation—it's the etiquette-appropriate way to let guests know where you're registered.

☐ update your registry two weeks before the wedding.

Add additional items if the supply gets low.

☐ keep a log of all gifts received.

Combine this list with a master guest list spreadsheet, so you have addresses handy.

☐ write thank-yous as soon as you receive a gift.

Writing a few at a time makes the task more manageable. Ettiquette states that you have two weeks to write a thank-you note for gifts received before the wedding; one month for gifts received after.

THANK-YOU NOTE SAMPLES

Sample thank-you note for a cash gift:

DEAR AUNT SUE AND UNCLE FRANK,

Thank you so much for your generous gift. Lila and I are saving for a new home and thanks to you, we'll be shopping for our dream house very soon. Again, many thanks for thinking of us and for sharing our special day.

LOVE, DEREK AND LILA

Sample thank-you note for a gift chosen from your bridal registry:

DEAR ELIZABETH AND ALBERT,

Thank you so much for the crystal wine goblets. We now have a complete set! Derek and I are looking forward to your next visit, when we can enjoy a drink together. Thank you again for thinking of us at this special time in our lives.

WARMEST REGARDS, LILA AND DEREK

Sample thank-you note for a gift you really didn't like:

DEAR WINONA AND LEIF,

Thank you for the fluorescent lava lamps. You are both so thoughtful! Every time we look at them, we will think of you and this special time in our lives. Again, many thanks for sharing our joy.

FONDLY, LILA AND DEREK

the honey moon

{ chapter 16 }

Before you can leave for your dream honeymoon, you (obviously) need to decide where to go. Whether it's mai tais on the beach or sipping bordeaux in Provence, you need to find a spot that suits your honeymoon style—both your styles. Get ready to learn how to pinpoint the perfect honeymoon spot and plan your trip.

researching honeymoon destinations

Honeymoons aren't always synonymous with beaches. Choose a place that suits your travel tastes and your fiancé's, whether it's hiking in the Andes or shopping along the Seine. Ask yourselves:

→ **when do we want to go?**

If your ideal spot happens to be a rainy mess during the month you wed, you may consider postponing your honeymoon until the weather is expected to be better.

→ **do we want to be cold or hot?**

Do you have to have snowy slopes, good for skiing and cuddling by a fire? Perhaps you prefer sunny-all-day-everyday weather, good for the pools or the beach.

→ **do we have budget constraints?**

If your wedding has taken most of your extra cash, you might consider a domestic location or a spot popular for its bargain flights.

→ **what activities are we interested in?**

If you're more the museum-going types, you'll be happy in a classical European city; but if you're more the hiking and nature types, you might consider a place like Peru.

→ **are there must-see places for either of us?**

If you have your heart set on a certain destination, talk it over to decide whether it's honeymoon appropriate.

→ **do we want to see a number of places, or stay in one place?**

If you pick multiple destinations, just make sure you have enough time at the first stop to adequately rest from the wedding excitement.

→ do we want to stay put or see the sights?

If you don't want to have to ride a train or rent a car once you arrive, make sure to pick a place with public transportation or a hotel within walking distance of everything.

→ do we want to use a travel agent?

A travel agent is a huge help if you're planning to hit multiple destinations, visit a foreign country, want inside info, or simply don't have time to plan a trip.

☐ get recommendations.

- Ask friends for honeymoon-spot suggestions.
- Log onto TheKnot.com/talk or TheNest.com/blog and chat with other couples about their honeymoons.

☐ decide on a destination, but before you do, confirm the following:

- Will we need to be concerned about drinking the water, foods, or any other safety issues?
- Will we need any immunizations?
- Do we need a passport, visa, or other documents?
- Is there a hotel there that fits our needs?

TOP 10 DESTINATIONS

and the best time of year to go

- Hawaii
  Best Months: all year!

- Bahamas
  Best Months: November to April

- Bermuda
  Best Months: May to October

- Caribbean
  Best Months: December to May

- Europe
  Best Months: May to October

- Florida
  Best Months: March, April, October, and November

- Las Vegas
  Best Months: March, April, October, and November

- Mexico
  Best Months: October to May

- Southeast Asia (Bali, Thailand)
  Best Months: October to February

- South Pacific (Fiji, French Polynesia)
  Best Months: May to October

why is it
called a
honeymoon?
Ancient Teuton
weddings were held
under a full moon
and afterward, the
couple would drink
honey wine for
thirty days.

organizing your trip

☐ decide how long you're going to be away.

See how much time you can take off of work and ask early for the days.

☐ research where to stay.

Scope out hotel websites in the area and check out the following:

- Price
- Room amenities
- Hotel amenities
- Proximity to surrounding attractions

☐ reserve a room.

Be sure to ask the following questions:

- Can we request the following items?
  - ☐ Room with a view
  - ☐ Room with a patio or terrace

BEST TRAVEL WEBSITES

Hit the Net way before you step on the plane.

- **BodyClock.com:** Use this jet-lag calculator to figure out what time you should go to bed to beat sleepiness.
- **DesignHotels.com:** A collection of hotels that have amazing design and décor. Search for spots in dozens of countries and book a room right through the site.
- **Grindskipper.com:** Get the down-and-dirty (along with info on cool clubs, stores, and hotels) on any urban destination.
- **Flight001.com:** Get stylish travel essentials like luggage, gadgets, and carry-on comfort packs.

- **InsureMyTrip.com:** Pick from an array of insurance policies and get quotes from 18 different companies to protect your travel plans.
- **Kayak.com:** An easy-to-use way to find cheap airfare.
- **LuggageForward.com:** Don't worry about lugging your suitcases to the airport—use this service to ship so they're at the hotel when you arrive.
- **TripAdvisor.com:** Read travelers' reviews and see ratings for tons of hotels and destinations.

- ☐ Bed size
- ☐ Private bath

- Are there any meals included with the room rate?
- Will we need to rent a car to get around from the hotel?
- What are the amenities in the room?
- What other amenities does the hotel have?
- Is there room service?
- Can we rent equipment from the hotel (snorkeling gear, skis)?
- What's the cancellation and refund policy?

☐ search for flights and rental cars.

- Search major travel websites like Orbitz.com and Expedia.com for price comparisons. You can often get discounts for booking a flight and rental together.
- If you have points or miles, call your airline to ask about blackout dates and reward seat availability.
- Sign up for updates and deal trackers to find discounts and deals.

☐ book your flights.

Be sure to ask:

- What are the terms for changing the date or time?
- What is the cancellation policy?
- Is there a frequent flier program we can join?
- Can we get our seating assignments beforehand?
- Can we request special extras for the flight?

☐ if necessary, book your rental car.

Be sure to ask:

- What are the car size options?
- What comes standard and what can we upgrade to?
- How does payment work?
- What's the cancellation policy?

☐ if you're traveling to a foreign country, decide how you're going to handle your money.

- Traveler's checks (find out if they're widely accepted)
- ATMs (ask your bank about fees; in many foreign countries they're extremely high)
- Foreign currency (consider exchanging $100 at your bank before your trip in case you can't find an open exchange window when you arrive)

☐ alert your credit card companies to your travels.

Call the fraud prevention department and let them know you'll be using the cards out of the country. Otherwise, they may not authorize your charges.

☐ sign up for travel insurance.

For the nominal fee, it's worth the peace of mind. Particularly if you are purchasing an expensive, nonrefundable package trip like a cruise or a tour.

☐ book popular activities.

Make appointments for spa treatments, private cruises, and the like—anything that you'd be disappointed if you weren't able to do.

☐ make dinner reservations.

This may sound a little overeager, but if you're traveling to a popular town, or if there's a hidden gem that has only six tables, it's worth it to secure a seat ahead of time.

finalizing the details

Packing can seem like a formidable task—especially when you have to pack days, or even a week, in advance. But trust us, you'll be so much happier to have a suitcase ready to go than to be searching for your bikini on a champagne buzz.

☐ put the following at the top of your packing list—
and check it twice!

- Airline tickets or e-ticket confirmation
- Passport/visas/driver's license
- Credit cards (take only those you'll need)
- Hotel/theater reservation confirmations
- Rental car confirmation
- Traveler's checks
- Two sets of photocopies of all the above, plus a photo-copy of related medical and/or trip insurance coverage and prescriptions (carry one set with you, and leave the other in the hotel room)
- Phone numbers for your doctor, house/pet sitter, and credit card companies
- Prescription medication (in the original bottle)
- Contraception
- ID tags for luggage
- Clothes (naturally)

☐ make sure to bring these must-haves.

Don't wait to buy these items. And if you don't plan to check your bags, make sure to look into the carry-on restrictions.

- Camera
- Film/memory card
- Extra camera
- Insect repellent
- Sunscreen and lip balm
- Sunglasses
- Sun hat or baseball cap
- Sunburn relief
- Band-Aids
- Pain reliever
- Antacid
- Antihistamine
- Diarrhea medicine
- Motion-sickness medicine
- Tampons/pads

- Paperback books
- Deck of cards
- Canvas tote bag for beach or pool
- Guidebook
- Electrical converter/adapter (if necessary)

☐ take care of the bathroom basics.

- Travel-size toothpaste
- Toothbrushes
- Deodorant
- Cosmetics
- Makeup remover
- Cotton balls and swabs
- Comb/brush
- Hair products
- Nail file/clippers
- Shaving cream
- Razors
- Contact lenses, solution, storage case
- Hair accessories

☐ find out whether your hotel will provide the following:

- Shampoo and conditioner
- Body lotion
- Hair dryer
- Alarm clock

☐ consider taking these extras.

- Extra pair of glasses/contacts
- Ziplock bags (all sizes; for wet swimsuits or protecting camera and film when it rains)
- Sewing kit
- Travel-size stain remover
- Antibacterial liquid or lotion
- Visine
- Small bag for day excursions and outings
- 1 pair old sneakers that can get wet or ruined
- 1 pair workout shoes; 2 or 3 workout outfits

- Swiss Army knife
- Compact umbrella or rain ponchos

☐ leave the following with family and friends.

- Your itinerary and hotel phone numbers
- Photocopies of your passport, credit cards, and traveler's check receipts
- A sealed copy of wills, life-insurance-policy numbers, and pertinent financial information—sounds scary, but it's just smart to do.

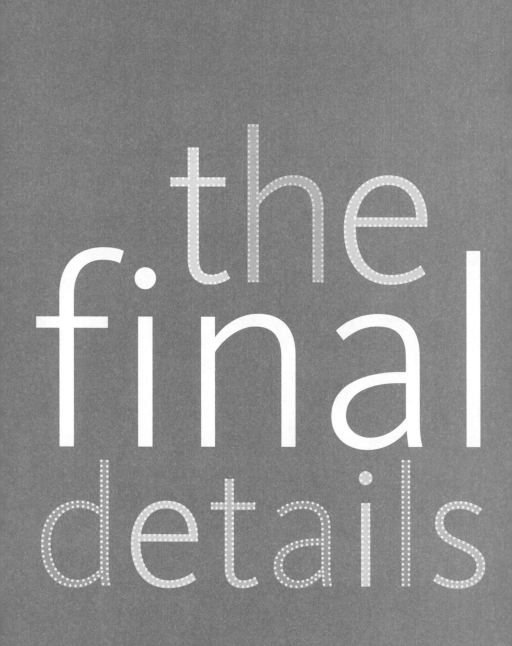
the final details

{ chapter 17 }

After all that planning and preparation, the most important thing you do on your wedding day is relax and enjoy yourselves. Take a look over our wedding day checklist and then toast yourselves—you're almost there!

the week before

Accomplishing these quick tasks will ensure a smooth-sailing wedding day.

☐ get a marriage license.

☐ prepare a weekend timeline of events. Distribute it to key vendors like the photographer and bridal party. Include:

- Key guest arrival times
- Transportation pickups and drop-offs
- Beauty appointments
- Any events that should be documented or attended (photo sessions, toasts, first dance, cake cutting)

☐ prepare an emergency contact list.

Include cell phone numbers for these VIPs:

- Bride's parents
- Groom's parents
- Maid of honor
- Best man
- Bridesmaids
- Groomsmen
- Child attendants and their parents
- Ceremony site
- Officiant
- Wedding planner
- Reception site
- Bridal salon
- Formalwear shop
- Ceremony musicians
- DJ/band
- Caterer
- Florist
- Photographer
- Videographer
- Cake baker
- Limousine
- Hotel

☐ deliver your seating chart.

Confirm any last-minute changes and hand off that final list to your reception site for setup and to take care of any seating mishaps.

☐ prepare a "day-of package" for each vendor.

Note any last-minute requests you have made. Also include items they will need in case they forget their copies (like the playlist for the DJ, special food requests for the caterer, and a family portrait list for the photographer).

☐ confirm your wedding night hotel.

☐ coordinate any airport pickups for close friends and relatives.

☐ review registry and make additions if gift options are running low.

☐ pack for your honeymoon.

Go to Chapter 16 for the ultimate list.

☐ get tip money together.

☐ write and revise your vows (if applicable).

TIPPING GUIDELINES

- Reception manager: 15–20 percent of the reception bill (less if there's also a maître d')

- Maître d': 15–20 percent (less if there's also a banquet captain)

- Waitstaff: at least $20 each (have the maître d' distribute tips for you)

- Bartenders: $25–40 each

- Restroom and coatroom attendants: about $1 per guest

- Valets: about $1 per guest (or arrange a gratuity with management)

- Limo driver: 15–20 percent of total bill (to distribute)

- Delivery drivers: $10 each

- Hairstylist and makeup artist: 15–20 percent of the bill

- Have extra $10s and $20s for unexpected occasions

On the day of the wedding in Chinese tradition, the bride serves tea to her parents as a sign of respect and to thank them for raising her.

☐ create bathroom amenity baskets.

Or ask your planner or site manager to take care of it.

the day before

☐ confirm last-minute details with your vendors.

- Directions to and from the site
- Time of delivery and pickup
- Your day-of contact information
- Name of the point person during the wedding

☐ prepare your toast to your guests and hosts.

☐ check the weather and make any last-minute arrangements.

☐ pack a day-of emergency kit.

This could be a task for your maid of honor, but either way, make sure she knows about this and can access it on the day of.

☐ double-check that you both have all the essentials for your wedding wear.

- Veil/tiara/headpiece
- Jewelry (necklace, earrings, engagement ring, his wedding ring)
- Shoes
- Undergarments (strapless bra, slip, crinoline, garter, etc.)
- The four necessities: something old, new, borrowed, and blue
- Groom's accessories (tie, cufflinks, studs, undershirts, socks, etc.)

☐ make sure you two, your bridal party, and your parents have the complete list of contacts.

survival
- Cell phone (fully charged)
- Mini bags of pretzels or PowerBars
- Small bottles of water
- Tissues

health and beauty
- Asthma inhaler or other medication
- Dental floss
- Small brush or comb
- Travel-size hair spray
- Barrettes, bobby pins, ponytail holders
- Nail file
- Clear Band-Aids
- Tweezers
- Small scissors
- Breath mints
- Deodorant
- Tums
- Small mirror
- Pain reliever
- Tampons
- Smelling salts (for fainting episodes)

dress-related
- One big safety pin (if bustle breaks)
- Extra pair of stockings
- Superglue (for a broken heel)
- Stain remover
- Double-sided tape (a quick fix for hems)
- Static-cling spray
- Small steamer for bridesmaid dresses
- Sewing kit with white thread and bridesmaid dress color
- Chalk or ivory-colored soap (to cover unexpected dress stains)

the wedding day

If the wedding is in the evening, don't spend the entire day stressing and running around. Take some time to work out or just relax. Either way, try to get to bed at a decent hour the night before (even if you're not sleeping, you'll want to be resting).

☐ eat a high-protein breakfast.

☐ give your wedding bands to your maid of honor or best man.

☐ have your hair done.

Be sure to wear a collarless, button-down shirt so that you don't mess up your 'do once it's done.

☐ have your makeup done.

Remember to brush your teeth first.

☐ put on your gown.

Be sure to hit the bathroom first.

postwedding

Once the day is over and you've taken time to relax on your honeymoon, there are still a few things to wrap up.

☐ write thank-yous.

Make sure that every last guest who gave you a gift receives a thank-you card. Etiquette says that for gifts given at or after the wedding, you have one month after you return from your honeymoon to get them out.

☐ follow up with your vendors

If you haven't already, make sure all your vendors are paid in full and you have wrapped up all business with them. Send them thank-you notes as well.

MAID OF HONOR TO-DOS

Preceremony
* Keep bride and bridesmaids on schedule.
* Keep the emergency kit on hand for anyone who needs it.

At the ceremony
* Arrange the bride's veil and dress at the altar.
* Hold the bride's bouquet during the ceremony.
* Hold the groom's ring until the bride puts it on him.
* Witness and sign the wedding certificate.

Reception
* Keep your eye on the bride and make sure she eats, and drinks water.
* Give a toast, if you didn't at the rehearsal dinner.
* Play host—mix and mingle and make guests feel comfortable.

Postwedding
* Help the bride change after the reception.
* Makes sure the wedding gown is put away in a safe place.

BEST MAN

Preceremony
* Keep track of the groom and keep him on schedule.
* Call to confirm transportation arrangements for the day.

At the ceremony
* Hold the bride's ring until the groom puts it on her.
* Witness and sign the wedding certificate.

Reception
* Keep an eye on the groom and make sure he eats.
* Have a map and directions to and from all locations, just in case the driver gets lost
* Give a toast.
* Play host—mix and mingle and make guests feel comfortable.

Postwedding
* Make sure everyone has a safe ride home.
* Arrange cabs if need be.

☐ if you've decided to change your name:

- Request several certified copies of your marriage license from the county office from which it has been issued (as proof of your union).
- Start with your social security card. Call (800) 772-1213 or go to SSA.gov to find the nearest social security office.
- Change your driver's license. Go to the nearest Department of Motor Vehicles to do so. There, you can also change your voter and auto registration.
- Change your passport. This requires a name change affidavit from the county clerk's office.
- After you've made the big changes, here are the other places to call and update:

☐ 401K accounts
☐ Car insurance/registration
☐ Bank accounts
☐ Billing accounts (credit cards, cell phone, electric, water, gas)
☐ Club membership
☐ Dentist's and doctor's office
☐ Employment records
☐ Homeowner's/renter's insurance
☐ IRA accounts
☐ Leases
☐ Life insurance
☐ Loans
☐ Medical insurance
☐ Other insurance
☐ Pension plan records
☐ Post office
☐ Property titles
☐ Safe-deposit box
☐ School records
☐ Social security
☐ Stocks and bonds
☐ Subscriptions
☐ Wills/trusts

Acknowledgments

One last list . . . of people I'd like to thank:

☐ kathleen murray and anja winikka for helping turn our infinite wedding knowledge into bite-size pieces for busy brides.

☐ pam krauss, kathleen fleury, aliza fogelson, jennifer beal and the whole clarkson potter team for making sure every checkbox was actually important to check.

☐ chris tomasino for your inspiration and enduring support for **the knot** books.

☐ wedding planners and vendors everywhere for your help making TheKnot.com and this book so rich and detailed.

☐ the knot brides and grooms—for your constant questions, unique ideas, and undying love of lists!